THE BARBERSHOP SINGER

Inside the Social World of a Musical Hobby

Barbershop singing is often dismissed by its critics as merely an enjoyable hobby. Though long popular with both its public and participants, it has been relatively neglected in the field of music studies. Robert A. Stebbins demonstrates that barbershop singing is an elaborate and complicated form of serious leisure that provides its participants with distinctive lifestyles. *The Barbershop Singer* is a unique study of this significant musical genre, describing the social world of barbershop and exploring its appeal for both male and female singers. Robert Stebbins traces the history of barbershop singing and compares and contrasts the worlds of jazz, classical music, and barbershop as serious leisure pursuits. Stebbins also examines its costs and rewards, its complex organizational structures, the social marginality felt by its more dedicated participants, and the main problems facing the art today.

Although barbershop singing is clearly a circumscribed social world, understanding how it works expands current knowledge of the variant forms of social participation available to citizens of the modern world. *The Barbershop Singer* will be of interest to sociologists as well as those involved in the world of barbershop.

ROBERT A. STEBBINS is a professor of sociology at the University of Calgary. He is author of *The Franco-Calgarians: French Language, Leisure, and Linguistic Life-style in an Anglophone City* and *Amateurs, Professionals, and Serious Leisure.*

THE BARBERSHOP SINGER

Inside the Social World of a Musical Hobby

ROBERT A. STEBBINS

UNIVERSITY OF TORONTO PRESS
Toronto Buffalo London

Toronto Buffalo London
Printed in Canada

ISBN 0-8020-0844-5 (cloth)
ISBN 0-8020-7829-X (paper)

Printed on acid-free paper

Canadian Cataloguing in Publication Data

Stebbins, Robert A.
The barbershop singer

Includes bibliographical references and index.
ISBN 0-8020-0844-5 (bound)
ISBN 0-8020-7829-X (pbk.)

1. Barbershop singing – Social aspects.
2. Music and society. 3. Barbershop singing – Alberta – Calgary. I. Title.

ML3516.S84 1996 306.4'84 C95-933157-3

University of Toronto Press acknowledges the financial assistance to its publishing program of the Canada Council and the Ontario Arts Council.

This book has been published with the help of a grant from the Humanities and Social Sciences Federation of Canada, using funds provided by the Social Sciences and Humanities Research Council of Canada.

To Dad and the Notable Four

Contents

Preface

This study of the hobby of barbershop singing reflects substantially my personal lifelong involvement in American music and music as serious leisure. Even though I do not sing barbershop, the 'barbershopper's social world resembles my own musical world in many respects. In certain ways, then, this book is also an autobiography.

I grew up in Wisconsin and Minnesota in a family reasonably dedicated to music, a family where classical music and traditional jazz recordings often filled the air. My father was an enthusiastic barbershop singer, my mother an occasional pianist, and my sister, a somewhat reluctant follower of our mother's interests. Somewhere around age five I started piano lessons. Later, inspired by the possibility of playing in the grade school orchestra, I switched my musical allegiance to the violin. I liked the violin, I think in part because it put me in contact with like-minded souls in the same school orchestras with whom I could play chamber music on occasion.

Then I changed schools. The lure of senior high school athletics and the lack of an orchestra at the new institution combined to temporarily eclipse my career as a musician. I did attend several of the Jazz at the Phil concerts that Norman Granz presented in Minneapolis during the mid-1950s, where I heard such artists as Illinois Jacquet and Lester Young, about whom I boast today, but about whom I knew little at the time.

The impression made by jazz and its performers lingered and was rekindled while I was enduring basic training in the United States Army. On weekends I would listen to the pick-up groups at the post exchange; many of them played well. I began to fancy myself on the bandstand, and more and more I saw myself playing the double bass there, an instrument with which I could easily identify from my earlier years as a violinist. Not long after my release from the military, I started lessons with one of the symphony bassists in Minneapolis inspired by the possibility of becoming a jazz musician.

That happened, although not exactly as planned. I did eventually work my way into the Minneapolis jazz community to make a living from the music, an experience that I also found sociologically rewarding inasmuch as it became the observational basis for my master's and doctoral theses. I toyed with the idea of seeking a career in music for I was also progressing well in the classical field. When I wasn't studying sociology or playing in a night-club somewhere, I was rehearsing or performing with the Minneapolis Civic Orchestra.

The choice of a career – academic or musical – was not, in the end, a difficult one. From my research and experience in music, it was clear that jazz and classical musicians lead difficult lives and that I could play their music with less hassle as either an amateur or a part-time professional. Moreover, my graduate work suggested that my talents might actually be greater in the intellectual than in the artistic realm. I set off in 1964 to seek my fortune as a professional sociologist and an amateur or a part-time professional musician.

The first stop was Presbyterian College, a small, liberal-arts institution in Clinton, South Carolina, where a twelve-hour teaching load and a desire to publish seriously hampered my musical activities. In 1965 I moved to the Memorial University of Newfoundland in St. John's. When I arrived I was the only trained bass player on the Island of Newfoundland! I was immediately recruited to the local orchestra, and soon I was soon giving bass lessons, playing every Saturday at a jazz haunt, working in the pit orchestras of musical productions, and performing as a studio musician for the local branch of the Canadian Broadcasting Corporation. I played as an amateur in the St John's Symphony Orchestra, while serving as its principal and sometimes only bassist. I was, moreover, its first president. Through all this I observed sociologically, occasionally taking notes as I went about my various musical involvements. These were also the years during which I published several scholarly articles on jazz musicians and the jazz community.

In 1973 I left Memorial University for the University of Texas at Arlington. My interest in playing jazz declined towards the end of my Newfoundland days, mostly because of the late hours. But my interest in classical music was thriving, due significantly to the private lessons that I received from internationally reknowned bassist, Gary Karr, and to the expensive new instrument I bought. Knowing now that I had a ready calling card, I went straight to the best amateur orchestra of the day in the Dallas-Fort Worth Metroplex, the Dallas Civic Symphony. It is a university-community ensemble based at Southern Methodist University (SMU).

I was soon playing as a section bassist in a group similar in stature to the Minneapolis orchestra. The principal position was reserved for a bassist imported from the Dallas Symphony Orchestra, usually its principal. That post later became mine when budget cuts forced SMU to rely more exclusively on student and community talent. That was 1976, the year of America's bicentennial. I led the section – now staffed mostly by music students – in performing a variety of American compositions including some that were highly experimental. It was a baptism of fire to be sure but also a terrific lesson on the importance of amateur orchestras in American classical music, both as a training ground for future professionals and as an outlet for new works. During these years that I wrote my papers on amateur classical musicians and started my study of amateurs and professionals in art, science, sport, and entertainment that was to continue for the next fifteen years.

Shortly after moving to the University of Calgary in 1976, I again sought the best amateur ensemble I could find. That turned out to be the university's orchestra and a smaller university-community group that played new music. I also rejoined the American Federation of Musicians at this time so as to play the occasional classical music job around town, give school demonstrations on the double bass (the 'Bob and Bertha' show), and to perform with the Calgary Civic Symphony, which I joined in 1979. That same year I led the first tour to New Orleans' Jazz and Heritage Festival. Those tours continue to this day. They constitute the field portion of a noncredit course on New Orleans culture that I give in the Travel Study Program at the University of Calgary.

Then, in 1988, Max Kaplan invited me, as specialist in serious leisure and the sociology of music, to join a team of researchers to study barbershop singers and their music. First with the publication of the papers resulting from this project and then with the publication of this book, it seems I have come full circle. I have now returned to the musical environment of my childhood and, particularly, the rehearsals in our living-room of my father's barbershop quartet, the Notable Four.

In every community, starting with my brief stay in Clinton, I played in chamber groups, some of which met regularly and performed publicly, some of which formed spontaneously and played only for the enjoyment of the musicians. These are in addition to the nine symphony and chamber orchestras to which I have belonged since my Minneapolis days. Yet my range of experience is even broader. In St John's I played for a while with a symphonic band and with a choir (as accompaniment along with a piano), in Calgary with a fiddlers' ensemble, and in Arlington with a group who performed youth-oriented church music.

For me, life is rich in music and sociology and their fascinating interrelationship. Recently, for the first time in my adult life, I took leave from all active music making for an entire year while I served as President of the Social Science Federation of Canada. To this point I had always been able to integrate, even though minimally, my musical and professional interests. There was no doubt that I missed the music during that time. And writing about music is never a decent substitute for making it. But, in the final analysis, I would have it no other way. I consider myself truly fortunate to find in my leisure *and* my work the same rich and absorbing involvement that barbershop singers find in their hobbyist pursuit of one of America's original musical arts.

In the first chapter of this book I introduce the concept of the social world and then, to gain perspective, I compare the social world of barbershop with the social worlds of jazz and classical music. This sets the overall theoretical tone for the study that is presented later. I add in chapters 2 and 3 the historical and organizational milieux of barbershop singing. Chapters 4 through 6 report on the field study of Calgary barbershop singers, their leisure careers in the art, their motives for pursuing it, and the place of barbershop in their everyday lives. As in any serious occupation, problems have developed in barbershop; I address myself to some of these in chapter 7. Chapter 8 departs from the theoretical and comparative themes introduced in chapter 1 to explore the serious leisure pursuits of jazz, barbershop, and classical music as special lifestyles.

Acknowledgments

A number of people have helped in a multitude of ways to make this book what it is. Bill Massena and June and Terry Crowe provided important documents about and useful discussion of male and female barbershop singing in both the past and the present. Sharon Green of Sweet Adelines International and Joe Liles, Dean Snyder, and Gary Stamm of the SPEBSQSA contributed invaluable commentary as well as considerable factual information about the male and female sides of 'barbershopping.' Singers Don Clarke and Randy Peters read parts of the manuscript and sociologist Max Kaplan read an early draft of the entire work. Finally, it was my good fortune to benefit from the editorial wisdom and experience of Dr Miriam Skey. Their contributions and suggestions are deeply appreciated.

Permission to reprint parts of the following articles written by the author is gratefully acknowledged: 'Becoming a Barbershop Singer,' in *Barbershopping: Musical and Social Harmony*, edited by M. Kaplan (Cranbury, N.J.: Associated University Presses, 1993), 55–72; 'Hobbies as Marginal Leisure: The Case of Barbershop Singers,' *Loisir et Société/Society and Leisure* 14 (1992): 375–86; and 'Costs and Rewards in Barbershop Singing,' *Leisure Studies* 11 (1992): 123–33. The fieldwork phase of this study was supported by the Social Sciences and Humanities Research Council of Canada with funds administered through the Research Grants Committee at the University of Calgary.

THE BARBERSHOP SINGER

Inside the Social World of a Musical Hobby

CHAPTER ONE

The Social Worlds of American Music

The number of distinct musical forms created in the United States in this century is truly remarkable. Among those with international standing we find jazz, blues, rock, ragtime, barbershop, black spirituals, and country music, both hillbilly and western. This list suggests that America is the home of an extraordinarily large group of musically innovative people. Clearly, Americans have a penchant for music and for inventing new forms of the art when its old forms, including those imported from other countries, become inadequate in some way as vehicles for emotional and artistic expression. The principal thesis of this book is that, although many different conditions in American life act to stir, guide, and spread this special creativity, one important set of conditions has received very little attention – the cultural and organizational milieu, or social world, in which a musical innovation is adopted, sustained, and diffused.

My aim in this chapter is to develop a conceptual framework for analysing the social world of barbershop and to explore in detail sufficient for the purposes of this book the historical foundation of this world in North America. Special attention is given to the country where barbershop was born, the United States. First two broad ideas that will serve as a framework for this analysis are examined: serious leisure and social world. Then a brief, comparative, historical overview is given of the social worlds in the United States that fostered the development, maintenance, and spread of jazz, barbershop, and classical, or art, music. In this comparison I explore the diversity of the social worlds of these other two forms of American music so as to bring into relief the distinctiveness of the world of barbershop.

I have chosen jazz and classical music for this comparison for several reasons. Like barbershop they are complicated, largely collective forms of art music. And like barbershop they require many years of practice to perform them well. None of the three is popular in the sense of enjoying significant commercial appeal. Finally, there is some sociological literature, meagre though it is, on jazz, classical, and barbershop music. This comparison will set the stage for the rest of the book and for the extended examination of the social world of barbershop singing.

The Social Worlds of American Music

The sociological concept that comes closest to describing the cultural and organizational milieux of the music mentioned above is that of the 'social world.' After reviewing several related definitions that have been proposed down through the years in sociology, David Unruh developed his own definition:

> A *social world* must be seen as a unit of social organization which is diffuse and amorphous in character. Generally larger than groups or organizations, social worlds are not necessarily defined by formal boundaries, membership lists, or spatial territory ... A social world must be seen as an internally recognizable constellation of actors, organizations, events, and practices which have coalesced into a perceived sphere of interest and involvement for participants. Characteristically, a social world lacks a powerful centralized authority structure and is delimited by ... effective communication and not territory nor formal group membership.[1]

In a later paper Unruh added that the typical social world is characterized by voluntary identification, by a freedom to enter into and depart from it.[2] Moreover, because it is so diffuse, ordinary members are only partly involved in the full range of its activities. After all, a social world may be local, regional, multiregional, national, and even international. Third, people in complex societies such as

Canada and the United States are often members of several social worlds. Finally, social worlds are held together, to an important degree, by semiformal, or mediated, communication. They are rarely heavily bureaucratized and, owing to their diffuseness, they are rarely characterized by intense face-to-face interaction. Instead, members of a social world commonly communicate by way of newsletters, personal letters, posted notices, telephone messages, radio and television announcements, and similar means.

According to Unruh every social world contains four types of members: strangers, tourists, regulars, and insiders. The strangers are most accurately described as 'mediators,' to use Marcello Truzzi's terminology, and might include, for instance, music publishers and musical instrument manufacturers.[3] They play an indispensable albeit intermediary role in the production of the art but seldom number among the artists themselves, around whom the social world initially took root. The tourists participate only momentarily there in their search for entertainment, diversion, or profit. In music, most members of the audience can be classified thus. However, as we shall see in chapter 5, they play a far more important role than the label of 'tourist' implies. The regular members routinely frequent the social world; in music all the amateurs and the majority of the professionals are regulars. The remaining professionals can be considered insiders inasmuch as they are the men and women who are exceptionally devoted to the social world in question and who have committed themselves on a full-time basis to maintaining and advancing it.

Two propositions are missing from Unruh's conception of the social world and these are vitally important for many of the chapters of this book. Every social world also contains a highly specific subculture and this subculture helps interrelate what Unruh referred to as the 'diffuse and amorphous constellations.' In other words we find associated with each social world a rich and unique array of special norms, values, beliefs, styles, moral principles, performance standards, and the like. Only by taking these elements into account can we talk about such aspects as the different social ranks of the inhabitants of a social world, as Unruh does when he distinguishes insiders from regulars.

Howard Becker's conception of the 'art world' is, in its broadest expression, similar to Unruh's idea of the social world when applied to the arts.[4] My preference for Unruh's conception rests on its equal emphasis on all four types of members compared with Becker's narrower concern with strangers – to use Unruh's language – and their cooperative links with chiefly professional regulars and insiders. It will soon become evident that amateurs, hobbyists, and audiences also cut significant figures in American music. Still, it is Becker who described how new forms of music and other art (in a word aesthetic 'innovations') come into being within the framework of an emerging social world.[5] When jazz, rock, barbershop, and the others broke loose from the established musical forms of the day to take root in their midst, they did so within the newly emergent cultural and organizational milieux of each form. These milieux consisted not only of the artists themselves but also of a number of intermediary collaborators, or strangers (e.g., recording companies, music publishers, barbershop societies).

By way of illustration, consider that the social worlds of jazz and barbershop were nowhere in evidence when the first sounds of these two new musics were being heard. Rather, as these sounds began to coalesce into increasingly recognizable forms of music and the new forms could be distinguished from the older ones, the people collaborating in the new music began to coalesce into loosely organized social worlds with accompanying subcultures. At first only insiders lived there; they were nevertheless soon joined, as the music became more established, by regulars, tourists, and strangers, with each category being related to the others by the norms, values, beliefs, and other components of culture that were themselves in the process of crystallizing.

Whether at the time of the early pioneering by the first insiders or later, in the age of the more routine performances by their established predecessors, the three forms under consideration in this chapter – jazz, barbershop, and classical music – are highly social arts. To be precise, they are almost always performed collectively, with at least two people. The lone piano players and singers who perform in public for pay or pleasure or in private for personal enjoyment number among the few exceptions to this rule. Most of the time those who want to make such music must find a chorus, quartet, orchestra, or small ensemble in which to do so, whether as work or as leisure. Thus nearly all these musicians experience a built-in dependency on others in their social world, a condition that cannot help ensuring its persistence.

The latter part of this chapter centres on several different aspects of the social worlds of jazz, barbershop, and classical music. Whereas experimentation with new styles continues in all three, the studies cited in this discussion were conducted long after the forms themselves had become well-established. As already noted, the first two are original to the United States and have evolved through the process of artistic innovation to the point where they are now world arts. The third, an import from Europe to which American composers have made many distinctive contributions, is a music whose styles are usually seen as transcending national boundaries.[6] Still, in its amateur sphere the social world of classical music has some properties that appear to be American in origin. The same can be said about barbershop, which is wholly leisure, and about the amateur side of jazz.

Music as Serious Leisure

Serious leisure is the systematic pursuit of an amateur, hobbyist, or volunteer activity that participants find so substantial and interesting that they launch themselves on a career, centred on acquiring and expressing its special skills, knowledge, and experience.[7] Amateurs, who perform the same activities as their professional counterparts, are found in jazz and classical music and, more generally, in art, science, sport, and entertainment. Hobbyists are enamoured of interests not presently pursued by professionals: collecting, making and tinkering, engaging in certain complex activities, playing certain sports and games, and acquiring knowledge for its own sake in one of the liberal arts.[8] According to the serious leisure perspective, barbershop singing can be classified as a hobby. Volunteering is defined elsewhere in this book as pleasant voluntary individual or group activity that is oriented towards helping oneself or others or both, is freely chosen, and is not done primarily for monetary or material gain. Career volunteering, which should not be confused with one-time or sporadic gifts of money, goods, or self (e.g., blood, organs), is conducted in a range of groups and organizations in the sectors of health, education, leisure, religion, politics, welfare, and in the larger community.

But serious leisure has other defining qualities besides the opportunity to pursue a career and acquire special skills, knowledge, and experience. It is further defined by the occasional need to persevere at it, as the amateur musician does when preparing a solo. Additionally, these pursuits produce many durable benefits, notably self-actualization, self-enrichment, self-expression, re-creation or renewal of self, feelings of accomplishment, enchancement of self-image, and attractive social interaction and group membership. Each serious leisure activity tends to generate its own social world within which it is pursued and with which participants come to identify, often quite strongly. As worklike as serious leisure might appear from all that I have just said, it nonetheless squares with the usual definitions of leisure.

Although the following chapters will demonstrate these qualities of serious leisure in many different ways, certain durable benefits are particularly prominent in jazz, barbershop, and classical music and therefore bear mentioning at this point in our overview. The benefits of enrichment, expression, and renewal of self are especially strong in these arts because of the vivid 'flow experience' they can provide for those who perform them.[9] When in flow while performing, the person's awareness merges with the action of creating the music to form a single sensation. Attention comes to be centred exclusively on the all-absorbing process of producing the music. A person in flow tends to lose his or her sense of self and to become wrapped up in the musical action of the immediate present. This state of mind is only possible when the conditions for making jazz, barbershop, or classical music are ideal or close to it, when the group is 'cooking,' as jazz musicians say. It follows that flow is autotelic; in other words the activity is intensely rewarding in and of itself. Chapter 5 contains a detailed application of the concept of flow to barbershop singing.

Since the three forms of music being considered in this chapter are most accurately and effectively analysed as either hobbyist or amateur-professional activity, career volunteering will receive only sporadic attention in this book. The amateur's relationship to his or her professional counterpart is, however, a matter in need of further explanation. In examining this relationship it becomes clear why barbershop singers must be classified as hobbyists, notwithstanding the excellence of some of their quartets and choruses.

Amateurs and Professionals

Professionals are often defined in common sense by two facts – they gain at least 50 per cent of their livelihood from their pursuit and they spend more time at that pursuit than amateurs do. This is of little real help in understanding the essence of either type. Since I have fully defined musical amateurs elsewhere, it must suffice here to note the following: Both amateurs and professionals can be more profoundly defined in comparison with each other as members of highly evolved professional-amateur-public (P-A-P) systems of relations and relationships.[10] This systemic definition effectively places both types in the same social world, which is organized around their common pursuit. Here they find special dependencies, career links, and patterns of interaction, all of which intersect with a common public, or audience.

Amateurs are facsimiles of professionals in a way, not only in music but also in the other arts and in science, sport, and entertainment. For instance, they engage in the same kinds of activities. Furthermore, amateurs are not necessarily inferior to their professional counterparts, even though the highest levels of achievement in their pursuits are nearly always reached only by the latter. Both types possess considerable skill, knowledge, and experience in their areas of expertise. Finally, most amateurs and professionals are *amators*; they love their activities so intensely that they can hardly imagine life without them.

As their membership in the P-A-P system implies, the professionals in question are oriented towards a public. Instead of providing a service to clients, as lawyers, physicians, and social workers typically do, public-centred professionals offer a work or a production to consumers. The work or production could be a game, exhibition, scientific study or, in music, a show, concert, or set of tunes performed in a night-club. By contrast, client-centred professionals specialize in treating, counselling, advising, diagnosing, registering, and performing similar services typically directed to individuals or individual organizations.

It should be evident by now that amateurs can only share a social world with public-centred professionals. The latter, even if they would have it otherwise, are unable to control the market for their works and productions. Amateur jazz and classical musicians, for example, perform for their publics sometimes for free and sometimes for pay and there is little that the professionals in these arts can do about it. Such arrangements are unheard of in the client-centred professions, where licensing and certification are carefully regulated by the professionals themselves and training is made available only to a select few. Put otherwise, the celebrated power of today's professionals as described, for instance, by Richard Hall and Douglas Klegon is in reality held only by those who serve clients.[11] Modern democratic societies have granted these men and women monopolistic control over training and services in such problematic areas of life as physical and psychological health. The work of musicians and, for that matter, of artists, athletes, scientists, and entertainers is not usually viewed as solving such lofty problems.

I have inserted this excursus about amateurs and professionals to show that, sociologically speaking, today's professionals are in reality very different from their common-sense, time-and-money definitions presented at the beginning of this section. Thus, when I argue in chapter 4 that barbershop singers are hobbyists rather than amateurs and that therefore they have no professional counterpart, it is the professional as described in this section who is missing. And I hope it is now clear that this missing person is significant. In barbershop, full-time professional singers are unavailable as role models, pace-setters, and experienced teachers. Nor do barbershop hobbyists have a professional career to which they might aspire as a way of slaking their insatiable thirst for their serious leisure.

American Music: Three Social Worlds

The focus of this book – the social world of barbershop singing – can be brought into sharper relief by comparing it with the social worlds of two of its closest neighbors in American music. To this end, a short overview of the social worlds that have sprung up around jazz, classical, and barbershop music is presented here. Each overview is introduced by a brief definition of the music being considered in an effort to distinguish it conceptually from the other two. But first, two cautionary notes. First, this treatment is necessarily sketchy when compared with what could be written about such complex subjects. Space limitations necessitate this brevity. Second, written definitions and descriptions of jazz, barbershop, and classical music, such as those presented here, are poor substitutes for or, at best, mere aids to, the much deeper emotional understanding a person can gain from listening directly and extensively to performances of these arts.

Each overview consists of a short discussion of the style of the music it addresses, style being one axis around which any artistic social world is sure to be organized. In jazz and classical music where several styles have evolved, certain ones continue to be important rallying points in those two social worlds. Unfortunately, the word 'style' is tricky, rich in different meanings and poor in overall precision. Following Joseph Machlis and Don Randel, we shall designate as a musical style any widely practised method of treating the central elements of a form of music (e.g., structure, rhythm, melody), a definition that is similar to that of 'school' of music.[12] Musical styles usually dominate during particular periods of history. A given style embodies the goals and ideals of the form at that time and, at its efflorescence, teems with conventions well-known to its audiences and practitioners.[13] The routine social relations among those who frequent the larger musical world unfold within this cultural shell.

Jazz

Whereas there are many definitions of jazz and none is without controversy, the one in *Webster's Third New International Dictionary* is more descriptive than most and as such is well-suited for our purposes:

> jazz: American music developed from religious and secular songs (as spirituals, shout songs), blues, ragtime, and other popular music (as brass-band marches) and characterized by improvisation, syncopated rhythms, contrapuntal ensemble playing, special melodic features (as flatted notes, blue notes) peculiar to the individual interpretation of the player, and the introduction of vocal techniques (as portamento) into instrumental performance.

This diversity of musical forms and practices existed in the latter half of the nineteenth century in New Orleans, where jazz is widely regarded to have been born. The social world of jazz that emerged out of this ferment was centred on the typical New Orleans musician, who was and still is remarkably well-versed in a great variety of types of music and musical practices as a requirement of his or her occupational lifestyle.[14] These musicians played together in various working units to perform music for marching as well as for dancing, listening, and the promotion of particular products and services. Certain social conditions in the 1890s, among them the repressed Louisiana economy and a recently enacted restrictive racial code, ensured that artistic collaboration would cross racial lines, bringing creoles (mixed whites and blacks) into contact with pure-blood blacks. The former, whose earlier privileged status with whites had given them access to training in classical music, began to share this training with their black colleagues who were generally self-taught.

The unit around which the social world of jazz developed was the band, which tended to have a shifting membership. Indeed many of these units were little more than pick-up groups, playing one-night stands at the night-clubs located on the shores of Lake Pontchartrain, the bars and dance-halls scattered throughout the city, and, although much less often than commonly believed, the brothels operating in the city's legalized prostitution district, Storyville.[15] Within this milieu between approximately 1890 and 1910 numerous conventions began to appear as guides to playing rhythm and melody and to improvising around the latter. Improvisation around a melody or simple theme came to be the preeminent value of these musicians, who gradually began to distinguish themselves as players of a different music known among them as jazz.

From its early twentieth-century beginnings in New Orleans, jazz has expanded enormously, evolving through at least seven different styles, depending on how one classifies the artistic innovations that have occurred since. The styles are presented here by name, representative performers, and approximate date of origin as found in the classification developed by James Collier and Bradford Robinson:[16]

Dixieland-traditional	Sidney Bechet Louis Armstrong	1900–10
Swing Jimmie Lunceford	Benny Goodman	1925–30
Bop	Charlie Parker Bud Powell	1939–40
Progressive-cool	Chet Baker Dave Brubeck	mid-1940s
Mainstream-modern	John Coltrane Miles Davis	late 1940s
Free jazz (avant-garde) Archie Shepp	Ornette Coleman	late 1950s
Jazz-rock	Gary Burton Larry Coryell	late 1960s

According to Collier and Robinson, each style continues as a vibrant force on the contemporary jazz scene. Therefore each can still be said to have its own 'subworld,' to return to Unruh's framework, which overlaps with the subworlds of adjacent styles.

Buerkle and Barker's study of the New Orleans jazz community and my own of the community in Minneapolis provide detailed illustrations of the modern complexity of these subworlds and their place within the larger social world of jazz.[17] In these communities and others like them we find a mosaic of subworlds, composed of numerous overlapping sets of personal networks and working bands organized around full- and part-time performing opportunities of a casual or steady nature, realized in such places as bars, parks, restaurants, and concert halls. Structures of this sort exist locally, nationally and internationally with many links across the three levels. A complex and picturesque culture of special norms, values, beliefs, and the like overlays the entire subworld; musicians who have never met can still perform together effectively with no more than a few perfunctory remarks about which 'tune' to play and in which key to play it. Among instrumentalists even the latter question need not be asked most of the time for well-known tunes are usually executed in standard keys.

Classical Music

The definition of classical music is in no way as neat as the definitions of jazz and barbershop, wherein the definer attempts to set out in one or two sentences the essential properties of the art. And even though the latter two still suffer from the omission of certain key concepts, the definition of classical music, taken from *Merriam Webster's Collegiate Dictionary*, 10th edition, is even sketchier:

> classical 3 b : of, relating to, or being music in the educated European tradition that includes such forms as art song, chamber music, opera, and symphony as distinguished from folk or popular music or jazz.

Classical music, which is sometimes referred to as art music, is in reality far too varied stylistically to be described generically, as jazz and barbershop can be. The styles themselves are highly complicated and for this reason can only be summarily listed here as was done earlier for jazz. The classification is that of Joseph Machlis, who cautions that the cutting points demarcating each style are vague and continually debated:[18]

AD 350–600	Period of the Church Fathers
600–850	Early Middle Ages, Gregorian Chant
850–1150	Romanesque
1150–1450	Gothic
1450–1600	Renaissance
1600–1750	Baroque
1725–1775	Rococo
1775–1825	Classical
1820–1900	Romantic
1890–1915	Post-Romantic
1910–	Twentieth Century

Organization by multiple subworlds is less common in contemporary classical music than in jazz. Many amateur and professional musicians play a variety of styles and thereby belong only to the general social world of classical music. In this art, subworlds tend to develop only at the extremes, among musicians who are interested exclusively or nearly exclusively in an experimental substyle within twentieth-century music (e.g., electronic music, computer music) or musicians who are interested mainly in 'early music,' or music composed before the end of the renaissance period. It is common to find amateurs in the second set of enthusiasts but only rarely in the first set. In other words they are highly unlikely to be musical pioneers, although those who play in university and community orchestras may have to perform avant-garde works from time to time.

What classical music lacks in the way of proliferating social worlds – it is more like barbershop than jazz in this respect – it makes up for in the complexity of the global social world to which most of these musicians belong. This complexity for the amateur members of the social world of classical music found in urban America and, we may safely say, in urban Canada, has been illustrated by showing in considerable detail how their involvement in this world is organized.[19] How far the observations presented in these papers can be generalized for countries outside North America remains to be determined.

Those who inhabit the social world of classical music stand together on the common ground of intense passion for performing the art itself. This they do in standard ensembles (e.g., chamber groups, orchestras) using a range of conventions centred on written parts and visual cues given by a leader of some sort (e.g., conductor, concertmaster). In addition, players of particular instruments discuss training experiences, exalted teachers and performers, problems encountered in producing the music, interpretations of parts, and similar interests. Live and recorded performances of standard works by well-known artists and ensembles constitute still another rallying point in the art world of classical music.

Barbershop

The comprehensive 'Barbershop Arranging Manual' offers the following definition:

> Barbershop harmony is a style of unaccompanied vocal music characterized by consonant four-part chords for every melody note. Occasional brief passages may be sung by fewer than four voice parts.
>
> The voice parts are called Tenor, Lead, Baritone, and Bass. The melody is consistently sung by the Lead, with the Tenor harmonizing above the melody, the Bass singing the lowest harmonizing notes below the melody, and the Baritone completing the chord either above or below the melody.[20]

Many authorities believe that barbershop song evolved into its present form during the latter half of the nineteenth century. Among its antecedents were the harmonies of the classical music of the day, the music of the Romantic period.

It is recognized, although not widely, that in the beginning black and white men and women sang these songs. 'The earliest occurrences of singing in a style one could call barbershop harmony probably came in the mid-1800s, perhaps improvised by plantation workers or by waiting customers in a small town barbershop as they sat idly, waiting for a haircut. Some elements of the style could be found in the singing of the Hutchinson Family Singers, a popular concert quintet with rotating family members, touring the country from 1840 to the 1880s.'[21] Barbershop was also sung by other travelling families of singers as well as by the quartets working in the minstrel shows of the period. It was also sung in various sized units in gospel music, both black and white. Those who presented their art publicly, although talented, were like those who sang it privately; in general these singers were untrained. Therefore they used nothing other than their own good ears to produce a balanced, close harmony.[22] Popular improvisation of harmony around a melody is possible only if the melody is simple and the harmonies are consonant. Many of the familiar songs of the late nineteenth century met these two criteria.

According to Val Hicks, the Golden Age of Barbershop got under way during the Gay Nineties and continued through the Roaring Twenties, a period that included the 'peak years' between approximately 1910 and 1925.[23] A declining interest in barbershop singing in the 1930s led to the founding in 1938 of the all-male Society for the Preservation and Encouragement of Barber Shop Quartet Singing in America (SPEBSQSA). Inspired by this initiative female barbershop enthusiasts established within the next ten to twenty years two societies of their own. All three societies have since become international, inasmuch as their art has now spread from the United States to a number of other countries. The organizational development of barbershop after 1938 will be considered in the next two chapters.

Although accounts of the era are woefully incomplete, the early social world of barbershop must have included certain common elements. There existed a simple, albeit ubiquitous unit of social organization – the spontaneously formed quartets of singers who hung around the barbershops. This apparently was common. 'While shearing, he [the barber] could also pitch a soft tenor above someone's melody, called lead. Often a customer would chime in with a tentative bass. When someone else filled-in the chinks with a fourth part, baritone or bari, harmony reigned.'[24] At the musical level, the preference for simple melodies and consonant harmonies soon took root, as did the preference for tunes consisting of thirty-two bar refrains. The lyrics of these tunes contained themes reflecting the social attitudes of the day, which by modern standards were sometimes more than a little racist or sexist.[25] The most respected music was unaccompanied. Somewhat later, when barbershop took to the vaudeville stage and began to face the requirement of being entertaining, the values of comic humour and showmanship became as important as the value of a cappella singing.

As the remainder of this book demonstrates, the social world of barbershop has grown immensely complex over the years. Unlike jazz, barbershop seems to have emerged more or less at the same time in a number of different communities, most of which were in the Midwest of the United States. From the outset this made for an even more diffuse social world than that of early jazz. There is still only one social world in barbershop, however; the singers here, oriented as they are towards tradition, have yet to engender any new styles. Indeed the only apparent division in this social world at present is the one between quartet and choral singing, with most 'barbershoppers' performing either one or the other.

Conclusion

Although the social worlds of jazz, barbershop, and classical music tend to be all-absorbing, some amateurs and professionals still manage to find the time to participate in two of the three. Dual membership is most likely in the first and the third but is sometimes found as well between the barbershop and classical music worlds. Participation in both jazz and classical music is possibly more common today than ever, the long-standing mutual disrespect between the two having now dissipated for the most part.

Jazz, barbershop, and classical music are distinctly different forms of music, the distinction being reflected in the equally different composition of their social worlds. Yet they have in common three important qualities: each is highly complicated, largely concerted, and generally noncommercial. No other form of American music can be described in these terms. Furthermore, as near as I can tell, no other form has engendered a social world that even approximates the social worlds that have emerged around jazz, barbershop, and classical music.

These social worlds have not been extensively studied. But of the three, barbershop has been neglected in this regard. One aim of this book is to help correct this imbalance in our understanding of one of America's three most substantial musical arts.[26] Notwithstanding its shared ground with the other two, barbershop also stands apart from them in three main ways – as a musical art, as a social world, and as a leisure activity. The distinctiveness of barbershop commands our attention. Let us turn first to its history.

CHAPTER TWO

The Old Songs

Much more could be written about the early days of barbershop than I wrote in the preceding chapter. This would lead into a more technical discussion of the art's past than could be justified here. The aim of history chapters in ethnographic studies like this one is to give only enough detail of the historical past to help the reader understand the sociological present. We have here, then, a question of balance. The present has depth for it came from somewhere and is going somewhere. An analysis of the present that ignores its past and future is like a performance of the second act of a three-act play for an audience who has come to see the entire piece.

Nevertheless this book is primarily about the present. Neither the past nor the future can be allowed to dominate. In this connection, let me note in passing that at least three important issues await the historian, issues from the past that continue to have an influence in the present. I will address these issues in subsequent chapters but they will be briefly introduced here prior to the main discussion of barbershop singing, which will take us from the founding of SPEBSQSA in 1938 to developments in the art in the 1990s.

Early Issues

One of the early issues revolves around who originated barbershop song and barbershop singing in the United States, blacks or whites? Lynn Abbott's study of the matter brings to light the tendency among white barbershop analysts to neglect the nineteenth-century practice of barbershop singing and the presence of barbershop harmony in black social life.[1] He gives considerable evidence of black involvement in barbershop, dating from that time to well beyond the turn of the twentieth century. His study helps offset the standard account of barbershop's antecedents, which, although not incorrect, is now clearly incomplete.

The account in question has it that barbershop singing can be traced to Elizabethan England, to the ballads of the day and to 'barber's music' sung by barbers and their customers.[2] Michael Dawney writes that in the seventeenth century, barbershops often had lutes available for the entertainment of waiting customers, who would play and accompany themselves in song.[3] In the eighteenth century these practices started to disappear in England, while across the sea in the United States they were just beginning to take root. Since so little mention is made of blacks in these histories, the reader gets the impression that these events must have taken place in an all-white society. Nevertheless, the black contribution to unaccompanied, four-part harmony, if not directly to barbershop, has been acknowledged. For example, Hicks wrote the following in 1988:

> The slaves on Southern plantations sang to make their life more bearable, to worship God, and to give vent to their feelings and moods. Their vocal harmonies were 'ear' harmonies ... After emancipation, blacks maintained this singing tradition, so that, as James Weldon Johnson tells us in a 1929 article in *Mentor*: 'Indeed, it may be said that all male Negro youth in the United States is divided into quartets ...' E.B. Marks relates in *They All Sang* that black quartet men would come to his Tin Pan Alley office to plug songs and seek work. They could harmonize skilfully, singing any voice part that was needed. Thus, according to these two men, both reliable sources, indeed, blacks were active and talented quartet singers.[4]

The black account of the origins of barbershop in the United States and the white account of its origins there and in England stress different aspects of the overall story. It remains for music historians to reconcile the two, exploring more thoroughly the relative contributions of both races to the art and its early development.

The second issue centres on the hobbyist standing of barbershop singers. I will explain this classification of serious leisure (as opposed to that of amateur) in chapter 4 as it relates to contemporary usage. By way of background note that in the late 1800s and early 1900s in vaudeville and later in the burlesque theatres and the Circuit Chautauquas, barbershop quartets were paid to sing. They were also paid by the major record companies to record their songs, which they did at first on wax cylinders and then later on standard discs.[5] When the microphone transformed the world of commercial entertainment in the late 1920s, the professional barbershop groups, with a few exceptions such as the Mills Brothers and the Maple City Four, began to disappear. The early microphones could not transmit the evenness of quartet singing. The popularity of jazz, radio, and sound films also contributed to this decline. Additionally, the widespread belief that barbershop was associated with the drinking and sexual excesses of the Roaring Twenties sullied its public image.

Does this development mean that at one time we had amateur *and* professional barbershop singers, whereas today we have only hobbyists? Not likely. Surely the number of employed quartets was small compared with the number of hobbyist quartets. It is highly improbable that a true profession developed around the former.[6] We do not even know how often the so-called professional groups performed for pay. Furthermore a number of them apparently abandoned a cappella singing between 1910 and 1920, when they discovered the commercial appeal of instrumental accompaniment. Once they made this transition their music could no longer be considered authentic barbershop.

The third issue is raised by Terry Gates, who ponders the value of parlour music in American society.

> What barbershoppers are really preserving, perhaps without knowing it, is even more valuable than their songs. It is not reflected in artifacts of words and music. It is reflected, rather in the human use to which they are put. Barbershopping, especially quartet singing, is arguably the last extant example in American culture of the ancient tradition of secular vocal parlor musics.[7]

Gates goes on to explain that parlour music is easily managed personal music which, when sung by a small group of people in the same room, produces interpersonal closeness. But why then do modern barbershop singers strive to perform in public festivals, large auditoriums, impersonal shopping malls, and similar places? The answer to this question lies, at least in part, in the role that a sizeable and enthusiastic audience can play in bringing out the best in these singers. Being swallowed up in a sea of barbershop song, surrounded by pure, ringing, consonant harmonies to which the audience avidly responds, is the most poignant thrill available for those who present the art in public.

The SPEBSQSA

The Society for the Preservation and Encouragement of Barber Shop Quartet Singing in America began as a local club, formed in Tulsa, Oklahoma, in 1938 by Owen C. Cash, a tax lawyer, and Rupert Hall, an investment banker. Although organizing a club for barbershop singing was a serious undertaking, its name and acronym were designed as a spoof on the proliferation in the 1930s and 1940s of government agencies known primarily by their initials (e.g., WPA, CCC, FDIC, and even F.D.R. himself).[8] According to Dean Snyder neither man had intended a national organization, only a regular occasion to sing in quartets 'the good old songs' (i.e., the traditional barbershop tunes, the old standards) that they remembered with great fondness from their younger days.[9]

Nonetheless, word of the new club and its first meeting spread quickly, resulting in a flood of membership requests from men who lived at some distance from Tulsa.[10] To protect its name, Cash incorporated it in late 1938. Around that time three new chapters were born, one in Kansas City, one in St Louis, where Cash had business friends, and then one in Hollywood, where Bing Crosby mentioned the organization during one of his radio broadcasts. With Hall as the first president of the 'Society,' as it is informally referred to, expansion continued from there to Chicago, Detroit, Cleveland, and Pittsburgh.[11] The Midwest has long been considered the heartland of male barbershop, where, at the time, the conditions for its resurgence could not have been better.

Chapters began to spring up along the east coast after Mayor LaGuardia unveiled his plan to hold an invitational quartet contest at the 1940 World's Fair in New York. Now there could be no doubt: the barbershop revival was under way, executed in typical American fashion by formally gathering all interested people into an association. Yet the revival was incomplete, for it failed to include all interested Americans. Blacks have never played much of a role in the SPEBSQSA (according to Abbott they were discouraged from joining during its early years), and women, being confined to a variety of nonperforming roles within the Society (see chapter 4), eventually started their own associations.[12]

The first SPEBSQSA singing contest, which was for quartets only, took place in Tulsa in June of 1939. The idea of the quartet contest had been around for some time. The New York Department of Parks had been organizing one annually since 1935, with ever larger numbers of contestants turning up each year. The American Legion in Oklahoma had also been holding contests.[13] One hundred fifty men came from seven states and seventeen cities to compete in the one in Tulsa. The event marked the beginning of the annual contest, now one of the most prominent features of the male *and* and female barbershop singer's life. The advent of the contest added a new dimension to the hobby of singing purely for the pleasure of making four-part harmony. Now barbershoppers could also sing competitively and sing to perfection (or at least aim at perfection) before a knowledgeable and appreciative audience. Clearly, the art's questionable reputation of the 1920s and early 1930s had been thoroughly cleansed.

The Society grew rapidly. Snyder reports that by 1941–42 there were perhaps two thousand members organized in fifty-five chapters.[14] These numbers were sufficient to justify a newsletter; SPEBSQSA's present-day bulletin, *The Harmonizer*, made its debut in 1941. The Society admitted its first Canadian chapter in 1944. By 1950 it numbered 26,900 members in 661 chapters spread across Canada and the United States. Although SPEBSQSA is a voluntary association and therefore hardly wealthy, it soon became evident that a set of full-time clerical and executive personnel was needed to serve the growing membership and to administer the increasingly large organizational structure and its ever expanding set of programs.

Expansion

A sudden drop in membership between 1950 and 1954 forced the leaders of SPEBSQSA to take action to save their organization from serious decline. Even though no one was ever able to identify the causes of this trend, the Society quickly adopted a number of major proposals that dramatically reversed it by 1955. In retrospect, it is clear that organized barbershop was changing during these years; it was evolving from its mission of establishing a fraternity of men who liked to sing and who enjoyed each other's company to this and much more. The following were among the proposals accepted for action at one of the meetings of the International Board of Directors held in 1954:

> 1) Enlarge the Society's purpose (which heretofore was simply 'to perpetuate the barbershop quartet ... and encourage good fellowship'); 2) Give training in music and barbershop craft to every member; 3) Elevate chorus singing to a greater prominence; 4) Embark without delay on a program of chapter leadership training; 5) Develop closer relations with local music teachers and choral groups and with allied groups in the arts and recreation fields and 6) Publish a professionally written text to explain and illustrate the barbershop style and choral arrangement in that style.[15]

Numbers 2, 3, and 4 were soon to become routine components of the lifestyle of the organized male barbershopper.

Although many contemporary singers are still unable to read music, 'woodshedding' (or improvising) the part they are interpreting would result in harmonic chaos were this done in a chorus. Accordingly, standard bass, tenor, and baritone parts are available today for all barbershop songs, and anyone intending to sing in the chapter chorus must know the appropriate part. In addition, local music training workshops are now provided regularly to help members develop their competency as singers. Finally, the devotee can attend the summer Harmony Education Program, which has been operating since 1961. Known today as Harmony College, the program, which is offered at a college in southern Missouri, accepts up to seven hundred students for a full week of instruction in singing technique, song arranging, ear training, sight singing, barbershop history, and more.

Although some chapters had established choruses in the 1940s, it was not until 1954 that the international convention saw its first choral competition. Now a chapter without a chorus is rare, whether it is a chorus of twenty members or two hundred. As for leadership training, it is available through the Chapter Officers Training School offered annually at the district conventions. In 1990 the Society instituted the week-long Directors College.

The 1990s

Today SPEBSQSA chapters exist in every province and state in Canada and the United States in more than eight hundred towns and cities. A recent 'fact sheet' states that the number of North American members stands at 34,649. From its headquarters at Harmony Hall in Kenosha, Wisconsin, the Society administers the male pursuit of a hobby of impressive international scope. Formal Society recognition is accorded to groups in Australia, Germany, Great Britain, Holland, Ireland, New Zealand, and South Africa. The global spread of nonaffiliated groups is, however, even broader. The Society recently formed the World Harmony Council, whose mission is to encourage and facilitate barbershop singing throughout the world. Each year it sponsors several exchange visits by touring quartets and choruses.

The SPEBSQSA of the 1990s publishes music, operates a reference library and museum pertaining to barbershop, and maintains formal ties with the Music Educators National Conference (in the United States) and the American Choral Directors Association. It also conducts a range of charitable activities, the most notable of which is its annual contribution since 1964 of increasingly large sums of money to the Heartspring School (formerly the Institute of Logopedics). The money goes for research and treatment of children with speech impairments, particularly where music can play a therapeutic role.

It appears that the globalization of barbershop song is destined to continue. 'It is expected that by the year 2000 one of the annual SPEBSQSA conventions, or an International Music Festival, will be scheduled to meet in London, England. Looking ahead to increased worldwide expansion, the Society's board of directors has rephrased its former motto, "Keep America Singing," to "Keep the Whole World Singing."'[16] On the whole, the crystal ball reveals a good future for male barbershop singing, though by no means one blissfully free of problems. The four most prominent problems will be examined in a later chapter.

Sweet Adelines International

It was June 1945. Edna Mae Anderson had just returned to her home in Tulsa after having attended that year's SPEBSQSA convention with her husband. During her journey she had come to her decision: she would organize an all-female barbershop chapter.[17] Owen Cash, his wife, and many of the wives of local male barbershoppers enthusiastically supported the idea. All agreed that it was most fitting that the first women's barbershop organization should take root in the same city where the men had started theirs seven years earlier.

An exploratory meeting was held in July at the Hotel Tulsa, the same hotel where the men had met to organize their first chapter. In August the Atomaton Chapter held its initial meeting as the first chapter of Sweet Adelines in America, Incorporated. Plans for starting a national organization by the same name began the next year, culminating in its premier national convention and quartet contest, held in October 1947. The headquarters of Sweet Adelines have remained in Tulsa since its founding.

Why establish another national barbershop organization? The most compelling reason for doing so is that women were, and still are in certain crucial ways, excluded from membership in SPEBSQSA. This practice is sometimes justified with the claim that in close harmony the differences in vocal timbre and range between the two sexes are incompatible. Still, a number of mixed quartets have been established over the years (e.g., Airwaves from Portland, Oregon), quartets which can only perform, not surprisingly, outside the jurisdictions of the male and female barbershop societies. In a promotional brochure, the Sweet Adelines organization goes about refuting this claim in its own way:

> For many years it was thought that barbershop harmony belonged strictly in the male realm, and that this type of singing was best suited to men's voices. Not so! Anything as nostalgic, as poignantly sweet, as romantically and historically interesting as barbershop harmony – anything as colorful and fascinating in the its costuming and dramatic possibilities was certain to have potent appeal for women.

It is also possible that the founders of the Sweet Adelines were inadvertently responding to cultural change. Terry Gates observed that in eighteenth-century America public singing was dominated by men, whereas today women are significantly more likely to be attracted to it.[18] The balance point was reached in the 1930s, a period during which both sexes were more or less equally enamoured of public singing. Moreover, as Sandra Parsons has noted, the 1940s and 1950s brought new freedoms to American women, including the possibility of independently pursuing their own distinctive hobbies.[19]

The Sweet Adelines rapidly grew to the point where a newsletter was needed. The organization's first and only organ, *The Pitch Pipe,* began publication in late 1949. Two years later the last part of the title of Harry Armstrong's tune 'You're the Flower of My Heart, Sweet Adeline' was adopted as the organization's official theme song. Then in 1953, a chapter was formed in Brandon, Manitoba, and though it failed a few years later, it did bring with it the first taste of international involvement. Thus there would have to be a name change: the 'in America' part was dropped, resulting in the denomination of Sweet Adelines, Incorporated.

The second half of the 1950s brought two critical challenges from competing organizations. The least problematic of these came from the short-lived Society of Women Barber Shop Quartet Singers in

America (SWBSQSA). The other challenge was born with the founding in 1959 of Harmony, Incorporated (see next section). This organization emerged as a reaction to the decision taken by the Sweet Adelines' Board of Directors to amend their bylaws so as to restrict membership in the Sweet Adelines to 'white women only.' The amendment was rescinded in 1966. Parsons said of the latter decision:

> It was an accomplishment to be proud of. The membership at large had brought about the change through constant reassessment and persistence. The International Board had acted in good faith with the original decision in 1958, and now they were again acting to remove the clause in respect of the members' wishes. The decision by the International Board was an honest reflection of the growth and intentions of the Sweet Adelines to truly try to harmonize *all* the world.[20]

As in SPEBSQSA the highlight of the year is the annual international convention and annual quartet and chorus contests. And like the men's organization a variety of instructional opportunities are now available by way of personalized training, weekend retreats, and group workshops. The Sweet Adelines has maintained ties for many years with the Music Educators National Conference and more recently with the International Society of Music Educators and the American Choral Directors Asociation. It has not, however, moved into the museum, library, and research fields to the extent that SPEBSQSA has. Nor does it support a major charity.

But the Sweet Adelines has certainly established its own global presence. This is reflected in the new name of Sweet Adelines International (selected in 1993) and the organization's motto, 'Harmonize the World.'[21] Most of its 29,603 members (as of 30 April 1995) are organized in over six hundred chapters distributed throughout Canada and the United States, with significant concentrations as well in Australia, Japan, the Netherlands, New Zealand, Panama Canal Zone, Sweden, and the United Kingdom. A spectacular fifty-year anniversay celebration was held in 1995 at the international convention in New Orleans.

Harmony, Incorporated

Notwithstanding its name, Harmony, Incorporated was a child of conflict among the members of the Sweet Adelines, Incorporated.[22] As just noted, that conflict centred on the decision taken by Harmony's board of directors to amend its bylaws in such a way as to restrict admission to white women only. Although many members of the Sweet Adelines were upset by this change, five chapters – four in New England and one in Canada – concluded that no further legitimate opposition to it was possible. Their only recourse, if they wanted to continue singing in a barbershop organization free of such restrictions, was to start one of their own. Accordingly the five chapters founded Harmony, Incorporated on 26 February 1959. The first issue of its official publication, *The Key-Note*, was published the following month.

Harmony's main reason for leaving the Sweet Adelines has become a source of enduring inspiration. In 1960 a member of Harmony wrote 'The Harmony Creed,' which the organization's board of directors accepted that same year as a replacement for its code of ethics:

Harmony from our hearts as well as voices;
Affection from each other oft expressed;
Radiant with our love of barbershop;
Mindful of our principles and ideals;
Outstretched hands to every race and creed;
Neatness in our dress and in our thinking;
Young in heart, for singing keeps us young;

Inspired with our desire to grow and flourish;
Nourished by devotion to our music;
Constructive in our work for Harmony, Inc.

The creed is still prominently exhibited in Harmony's promotional literature, even though the board voted in 1975 to reinstate the code of ethics in its place. In 1984 one of the members composed the twenty-fifth anniversary song, 'We're Harmony, We're Strong!'

It contains references to democracy and to 'one voice, one vote that is the key, all women can belong,' attesting once again an official readiness to avoid the high-handedness the Sweet Adeline board of directors was felt to have perpetrated in 1957 and 1958. Harmony's theme song, 'A Song of Friendship,' has lyrics conveying similar messages.

Harmony functions in much the same way as the other two barbershop societies. Indeed it has been advised locally and internationally by SPEBSQSA and, in several areas, has modelled itself after this organization. For instance it has developed along the lines of community-based chapters. It also holds an annual convention, whose centrepiece is the choral and 'quartette' competitions. Like the other two, each year Harmony gives a number of awards for excellence in singing, directing, and service to the organization, as well as for working up the best chapter bulletin and the best history book. The Harmony Training Program offers local instructional programs designed to improve barbershop singing. The Harmony Intensive Training School provides instruction in directing, judging, music theory, show production, quartet coaching, chapter administration, and many other subjects.

By 1964 Harmony had 511 members dispersed in sixteen chapters located in Ontario, Quebec, and the New England and northern tier states running as far west as Wisconsin. Today membership stands at about 2,200. Most of the chapters are still found in this same geographical area, although the society has recently seen considerable expansion in the Maritime region of Canada. At present its membership is limited to Canada and the United States. Harmony comes closest of the three societies to being purely a hobbyist group inasmuch as it has no formal ties with other musical and educational organizations and maintains no museum, library, or research functions. Nonetheless it does contribute annually to a major charity, the National Society for Children and Adults with Autism (in the United States) and the Autism Society Canada.

Conclusions

Despite the nearly equal size today of SPEBSQSA when compared with the combined membership of the two women's organizations, the male Society continues to enjoy the greater popularity and influence in the wider community. True, it has been around somewhat longer but a mere nine years difference in age does not seem to explain this difference in image. Rather the most convincing explanation probably lies in American popular culture itself and the long-standing belief that barbershop singing is ineluctably male. After all it can reasonably be argued that it was men, rather than women, who went to the barbershops in the nineteenth century where the art began in significant part. Moreover, men appear to have dominated the vaudeville shows and later the Circuit Chautauquas and the cylinder and disc recordings. And according to Gates, women sang less in public during these times than men.

What the nine-year gap did do for the men was give them a head start in organizing their art. During that period they set up the basic organizational structure and system of awards so familiar to us today. Although the elaborate training programs for singers, directors, and administrators had not yet been established, members of SPEBSQSA were nonetheless gaining valuable experience in these three areas. Thus in their early years both Harmony, Incorporated and the Sweet Adelines had at their disposal knowledgeable male barbershop singers who could serve as contest judges and chorus directors and advise them on various organizational and educational questions. Their published histories suggest that, in this connection, the men usually gave generously of their time and did so without condescension. Only recently have female chorus directors come to be the norm. Finally, there may still be a public bias favouring the lower sound of a set of male voices interpreting a barbershop song when compared with a set of female voices singing the same selection. It is what the public has become used to, what it expects when someone says 'barbershop.'

Organizations constitute an important part of the social world of barbershop. An efficient and effective organization can speed the evolution and diffusion of the established side of any art. There is no reason to believe that men are inherently better at founding and developing formal groups than women. In barbershop, however, they did get started earlier at doing this, organizing themselves in a way that was attractive enough for the women who followed to copy their innovations. Moreover, the men have somehow avoided the organizational fragmentation that has plagued their female counterparts. And notwithstanding the occasional talk in both female societies about a possible merger of the two, the schism remains.

CHAPTER THREE

Organized Barbershop

Not everyone who sings barbershop is a member of one of the three organizations described in the preceding chapter. Notwithstanding present-day recruitment efforts by the societies, many teenagers feel uncomfortable in the company of most barbershop singers, who are old enough to be their parents or even their grandparents. Apparently the feeling is mutual, for, at least in Harmony, Incorporated, a bylaw existed until 1983 restricting membership to those eighteen years old and over. But there are also adults who sing in quartets having no affiliation whatsoever with any barbershop organization. For a quartet to be affiliated, or in a more formal sense, registered, all members must belong to the same organization, a requirement that may not suit everyone. The reasons for eschewing organized barbershop will not be explored here. Our focus is on those barbershoppers who do belong to one of the three societies and who do make up the vast majority of all a cappella singers executing four-part harmony.

It is possible that barbershop singing is the most formally organized hobby we know. According to current research, collectors and makers and tinkerers usually construct comparatively simple social worlds, which revolve around local clubs or similar groups and which are sometimes loosely knit together by a regional or national society, association, or federation.[1] This research suggests that the local club is the true organizational nucleus of the social world of a particular hobby, whereas the umbrella groups are, sociologically speaking, more peripheral. For the most part people pursue their hobbies locally, while a devoted set of volunteers, whether elected or not, may come together at the regional or national level to carry out such functions as public relations and the coordination of resources and activities. It is the same for the activity participants and the players of sports and games, except that, where there are leagues and routine contests, the structure of the surrounding social world becomes somewhat more complicated.

I will justify my classification of barbershop as a hobby in the next chapter, where I argue that the art finds its home among the activity participants, whose interests are as diverse as sport fishing, bird-watching, and hang-gliding. The principal aim of the present chapter is to examine the formal organizational side of the social world of barbershop. This chapter also contains a case study of the extent to which a hobby can evolve in the sphere of complex organization.

Chapters, Quartets, Choruses

The chapter in organized barbershop is the equivalent of the club in other hobbies, inasmuch as it is the lowest common organizational denominator. Nearly everyone who is a member of one of the three societies is also a member of a *local* chapter. The only exceptions to this rule are the members of what I shall refer to here as a *catch-all* chapter (labelled differently in each society), an administrative arrangement for organizing members who are geographically mobile, who live in communities too small for a chapter, or who must leave barbershop temporarily.

My research suggests that every active member of the local chapter sings in either a quartet or the chapter chorus. The large majority of active members participate in the latter, whereas a minority, sometimes a small minority, routinely sing with a quartet, which may or may not be registered with the international organization. Most quartet singers also sing in the chorus, although some avoid this because they lack the time for both (each rehearses weekly), strongly prefer quartets, or are members of a catch-all chapter where no chorus is available. The 1993 Dieringer survey turned up a similar pattern of participation: 2.6 per cent of their sample sang exclusively in quartets, 72.2 per cent sang exclusively in choruses, and 21.4 per cent sang in both.[2] Whatever the pattern of participation it is in the local chapter (not the catch-all chapter) where routine contact with the social world of barbershop takes place and where the hobbyist gains access to the resources of the umbrella regional and international organizations.

But the hobbyist lifestyle of the local barbershop singer is more complicated than this. Chapter members also have service work to do and, whereas some of them manage to avoid it, all are expected to help in one way or another in this regard. Every chapter has a board of directors consisting of the chapter's president, vice-president, secretary, treasurer, and other key functionaries (e.g., chorus director, chairs of major committees). The following abbreviated list of committees demonstrates that together they cover a vast terrain: executive, nominating, membership, annual show, dress, music (selection of songs, auditions), and community service. In addition to the positions represented on the board, chapter members must be found to fill the positions of music director, section leader (of the basses, baritones, etc.), chapter bulletin editor, stage presence expert, chapter historian, and public relations officer, to mention but a few.

The SPEBSQSA's president's manual, written in 1989, described thirty-three chapter positions and committees and then ended by suggesting that the list was not necessarily exhaustive.[3] In 1989 the Calgary-based Chinook chapter of Sweet Adelines had twenty-six committees and half again as many positions. Thus there appear to be nearly as many opportunities of this sort for many of the women as for the men. The implications of such service work for the individual singer will be considered in the next chapter under the heading of the serious leisure career.

We will also examine more thoroughly in chapters 4 and 6 the reason all barbershop organizations have for existing (whether locally, regionally, or internationally), which is to sing unaccompanied, four-part harmony. In other words the chapters, quartets, choruses, positions, and committees are not ends in themselves but mere human social arrangements for facilitating a highly valued activity. As elaborately organized as modern barbershop is, then, all this organization is in itself of secondary importance when compared with the activities of rehearsing and performing in quartets and choruses. It is true that all chapter members enjoy immensely the social life that emerges when they make music together and smaller numbers of them like the challenges of service work. Still, all but a very few come primarily to sing. To quote from the Sweet Adelines promotional brochure: 'The chapter is the "workshop" where members receive their basic training in barbershop harmony while participating in their prime endeavor – singing!'

The barbershop singer who performs service work for his or her chapter or for a higher eschelon of the society is in that role effectively a volunteer rather than a hobbyist. In other words, he or she is engaging in another type of serious leisure and is therefore acting on the basis of motives distinctly different from those driving the hobbyist. Volunteering refers to pleasant voluntary individual or group activity that is oriented towards helping oneself or others or both, is freely chosen, and is not done primarily for monetary or material gain.[4] Volunteering is distinguished from amateur and hobbyist activities by, among other qualities, its substantial altruism. Although it is now well established that volunteers are typically directed by both altruistic *and* self-interested motives, altruism influences volunteers far more than it influences amateurs and hobbyists.[5] The second two pursue their leisure primarily for self-interested reasons.

Districts, Regions, Areas

All three international barbershop societies have carved up Canada and the United States into more manageable administrative units known as districts (SPEBSQSA), regions (Sweet Adelines), and areas (Harmony, Inc.). Presently there are sixteen districts and twenty-six regions. Harmony is composed of the four areas and their subdivisions, all of which have been established for some time, and twelve expansion areas. An expansion area remains under the jurisdiction of one of the four established areas until a minimum of five chartered chapters have emerged and it has developed its own Harmony Training Program and appointed a representative to the international organization. At this point it can become an established area in its own right.

Each district, region, and area is run by an elected board of directors, which sends one or more representatives to the meetings of the international body. Although these intermediate units are less active than the chapters, they still have plenty to do. In the main, they organize each spring and sometimes each fall a convention, in which the quartet and chorus contests figure prominently. Winners proceed the following year to the international convention and contest, held for the men in late June or early July and for the women in late October or early November.

The regional (district, areal) conventions, although hardly as elaborate as those of the international society, are nonetheless substantial undertakings. Everything revolves around providing within the span of a weekend the time and space for rehearsals and performances for large numbers of quartets and choruses. Seventeen choruses and twenty-six quartets participated in the competition that I observed at the 1989 convention of SPEBSQSA's Evergreen District. I observed another nineteen choruses and twelve quartets that same year at the convention of Canada's Maple Leaf Region of the Sweet Adelines.

The chapter sponsoring the convention shoulders the responsibilities for all local arrangements. Nineteen members in each chapter put in an enormous amount of time and effort to make a success of the two previously mentioned conventions. In and around all this the district or regional board of directors will convene two or three times, while the rank-and-file, when not rehearsing or performing, will arrange to meet old friends, visit the room where the barbershop merchandise is sold, and tour the city hosting the affair.

The International Societies

The international societies go to great pains to organize and carry out their annual conventions, which last a week and which many members regard as the main event of the year.[6] Especially for the men, whose convention unfolds during the most popular vacation period of the year, it is also likely to be a family affair. Activities are organized for wives and children, and families arrive in the convention city with plans for holidaying in the area afterward. As always the host chapter has its work cut out for it, as it goes about making hundreds of detailed local arrangements. This was what the Calgary chapter faced when it organized the 1993 SPEBSQSA international convention. Over 11,000 people registered for the event, making it the largest the Society had ever seen to that point and hence the most challenging to organize.

The international societies are a veritable mosaic of positions, committees, administrative divisions, and affiliated organizations. Except for an executive director and his or her remunerated office personnel (the Sweet Adelines has thirty-three, SPEBSQSA has forty-two) all are run and staffed by volunteers, nearly all of whom also want to devote some of their leisure hours to being hobbyist barbershop singers. Most members of the international committees can only find the time and money to meet once a year, with the annual convention being the most convenient occasion for this. The result for them is an extremely busy convention week. Paralleling the various contests at the Calgary convention of the SPEBSQSA were the meetings of over thirty committees and affiliated organizations. Understandably, the bureaucratic structure of one of these organizations grows in complexity as its membership expands. Complexity also increases when the organization takes on new functions deemed important to its mission.

The missions of the three societies are by no means the same:[7]

> Sweet Adelines International – The purpose of Sweet Adelines, Inc. has always been the education of women to sing four-part harmony, barbershop style, to develop an appreciation for this art form, and to give public and private performances.
>
> Harmony, Incorporated – An international organization of women who love to sing barbershop harmony. Members are pledged and determined to combine good governmental practices with barbershop harmony. Its doors are wide open to all who respond to the ringing chord.
>
> SPEBSQSA – The Society is to be a widely recognized, ever-growing, singing fraternity of men, drawn together by their love of the four-part, a cappella, close-harmony style of music known as barbershop,

> whose mission is to perpetuate that style by sharing it and their love for it with people of all ages throughout the world; and to be a leader in the cause of preserving and encouraging vocal music, in our education systems and in our communities, as a lifelong recreational activity and an essential element in one's cultural well-being.

The mission of the Sweet Adelines is straightforward: to provide musical education in four-part harmony and widespread appreciation of this art form. Harmony stresses the enjoyment of barbershop singing for all women and its pursuit using democratic procedures. The men's Society is guided by the broadest mission. It adds to those of education and appreciation, the additional goals of good fellowship, preservation of the art of barbershop, participation in charity, and individual and community musical development in the field of vocal harmony.

It is hardly surprising, then, that the proliferation of positions, committees, administrative divisions, and affiliated and subsidiary organizations has gone farthest on the international level of SPEBSQSA. It is to this society that we turn for an illustration of the structural complexity of the social world of barbershop singing in the 1990s, a complexity that will, however, be reduced somewhat in 1997 in the course of a major reorganization to result in the following:

SOCIETY BOARD OF DIRECTORS (15 MEMBERS)

- President
- Immediate Past-President
- Treasurer
- At-Large Directors (3)
- District-Elected Directors (8)
- Executive Director and Secretary (nonvoting)

COMMITTEES

- Special Events Committee
- Contest and Judging Committee
- Marketing and Communications Committee
- Laws and Regulations Committee

Barbershop Heritage Committee
Investment Advisory Committee
Chapter Support and Leadership Training Committee
Chorus Director Development Committee
Membership Development and Outreach Committee
Ways and Means Committee
External Affairs Committee
Music and Performance Committee
Ethics Committee
Nominating Committee
Heartspring and Service Committee (tentative title)
World Harmony Council

ADMINISTRATIVE DIVISIONS

Chapters Operations Training Seminars
Directors College
Fund for the Advancement of Musical Education
Harmony College
Harmony Explosion (school club program)
Harmony Foundation (charities and endowment)

SUBSIDIARY ORGANIZATIONS

Ancient and Harmonious Society of Woodshedders (improvisational singers)
Association of International Champions (quartets)
Association of International Seniors Quartet Champions
Confederate Harmony Brigade (casual singing organization)
Organization of Past International Board Members and Wives of Past International Board Members
NEWCANEWENG (casual singing organization)
DELASUSQUEHUDMAC (casual singing organization)
PROBE (P.R. officers, bulletin editors)

AFFILIATED ORGANIZATIONS

Australian Association of Men Barbershop Singers
Barbershop in Germany
British Association of Barbershop Singers

Dutch Association of Barbershop Singers
Irish Association of Barbershop Singers
New Zealand Association of Barbershoppers
Society of Nordic Barbershop Singers
Southern Part of Africa Tonsorial Singers

This organizational colossus, which includes several task forces, is run by the Society President, the Executive Director, the Society Board of Directors, and three functional units of the latter (Planning and Program Development Group, Operations Group, and Board Management Council). To my knowledge, no other hobby has an organizational structure this complex.

The Sweet Adelines is organized in an analogous albeit somewhat more complex way. It operates with a Board of Directors, whose twelve members are elected at large, and a Council of Regents consisting of one representative, or 'regent,' from each of the twenty-six regions. Harmony has a similar structure which, because of its smaller size, is the least complicated of the three. Although its Board of Directors also has some elected members-at-large, there is no council of regents.

Conclusions

When it comes to individual opportunities, the kind of formal organization described in this chapter both 'giveth and taketh away.' Thanks to the existence of the three international societies, barbershop singers can join established choruses, give public performances, enter efficiently run contests, and receive vocal and musical training, to mention just a few of the benefits. At the same time such participation is limited by the rules of the organization providing the resources for it. For example, chapter members must attend a specified number of choral rehearsals if they want to sing in the next annual show, quartets must sing authentic barbershop songs if they want to compete in their society's contests, and lyrics of new barbershop songs must now be free of sexist and racist implications if they are to be sung at society-sponsored events.

Thus becoming a barbershop singer today in North America and increasingly throughout the world means accepting restrictions of this sort. Pursuing a serious leisure career in barbershop means pursuing personal musical development according to official standards and pursuing organizational advancement through the channels of an established bureaucracy. It could be otherwise; a man or woman could enter the hobby and find a career there in ways substantially different from those described in the next chapter. A close look at the other variety arts and at the fine arts would reveal many alternatives. But it is unnecessary to go that far afield. In chapter 7 we shall see that some barbershoppers have already invented their own alternatives.

All this is not to say, however, that barbershop singers are dissatisfied with their leisure lot. Quite the contrary, they generally seem most pleased with the opportunities provided by the international societies. As for the restrictions, only a few even seem to notice them.

CHAPTER FOUR

Becoming a Barbershop Singer

The most central unit in the social world of barbershop is the local chapter, which promotes chorus and quartet singing in barbershop style. The typical chorus meets weekly in an evening rehearsal. Members of the chorus who also belong to a quartet commonly rehearse with the latter group during another evening or perhaps during the weekend. Maturity in chorus and quartet singing means, among other things, that these groups strive for such a level of excellence that they can attract the public to annual shows and shorter concerts of various kinds known in barbershop circles as 'singouts.' Even more demanding in terms of polish are the annual regional, district, or areal contests where panels of highly trained judges evaluate and rank each competing quartet and chorus. The winners advance to the ultimate competition, the one held the following year at their society's international convention.

This is the core of barbershop singing. The enjoyment of making music in the barbershop idiom is the central reason for participating in this form of leisure. But, as previously noted, scores of nonsinging activities also occupy the leisure time of most members of any chapter. Although peripheral because they do not lead directly to the production of music, these activities are nonetheless important as they support the music making. Thus members may participate in the administrative affairs of their chapter or region or district and, more rarely, in those of their international society. Costumes and uniforms are worn at contests and performances and members must either make or purchase them. Annual shows are often presented before a theatrical backdrop of some sort; this is almost always constructed by the singers. Committees or individuals are responsible for recruiting and auditioning prospective members, ordering and distributing new music, and organizing occasional workshops for individual and collective improvement. Still other committees are charged with show publicity, ticket sales, and social events. The latter include the annual banquets, Christmas parties, and 'afterglows' – the lively and lengthy receptions for insiders held after each show. They include ample food, drink, conversation, and, it goes without saying, quartet singing. Barbershop singers if they choose to do so can become heavily immersed in all this and more. It can become a main, and for a small proportion of members even *the* main, leisure activity in their lives.

The aim of this chapter is to explore how a sample of Canadian men and women became attracted to the core and peripheral activities of the art of barbershop. The data come from an exploratory study of the quartets and choruses of three chapters in Calgary, Alberta, as well as a small male splinter group of expert singers, which holds a 'licence' as a chapter in the process of developing. One main source of data was my direct observation of the principal activities of the chapters and the splinter group. This included travelling with them to their regional or district conventions.

The other main source was interviews with thirty-two singers, who made up a representative sample consisting of sixteen males (eight in quartets, eight in choruses) and sixteen females (same distribution) selected randomly from the membership lists of two of the four chapters. The scope of these interviews and hence of this chapter and chapters 5 and 6 is evident from the interview guide reprinted in the Appendix. I hired no assistants for this project. Rather I carried out my own observations and interviews over the fourteen-month period running from December 1988 through January 1990. The object of the study was to generate a grounded, or inductively developed, sociological theory of barbershop singing as serious leisure using the procedures of exploratory research set out by Glaser and Strauss.[1]

Barbershop as Serious Leisure

One of the principal assumptions underlying this study was that barbershop is a type of serious leisure for the large majority of its male and female participants. This is its scientific classification. Serious leisure was defined and described in chapter 1. As background for the observations reported in the present chapter, I should now like to expand on what was said there.

Serious leisure is leisure in which its practitioners encounter the occasional need to persevere, although this need is significantly less acute than in some occupations and significantly more acute than in its opposite, casual leisure. Moreover, a career awaits the serious leisure enthusiast. It consists of a history of turning points, levels of achievement and involvement, and a set of background contingencies. Third, personal effort is common in such leisure, as based on extensive skill, knowledge, or experience and oftentimes a combination of these. Those who engage in serious leisure derive various durable benefits from it, including self-actualization, self-enrichment, feelings of group accomplishment, and enhancement of self-image. Further, they find in connection with each serious leisure activity a unique social world composed of special norms, beliefs, values, morals, events, principles, and traditions. These five distinguishing qualities are the soil in which the sixth takes root: practitioners come to identify strongly with their avocation.

Amateurs make up one category of serious leisure participant. They can be defined by their many interdependent relations and relationships with a professional counterpart and with a public who is served by either or both sets of experts.[2] We have said that the second category of serious leisure practitioner – the career volunteer – engages in enjoyable and rewarding voluntary action (individual or group) that is oriented toward helping oneself or others or both, is freely chosen, and is not done primarily for monetary or material gain. For this person, volunteering is a long-term expression of skill, knowledge, or experience, or their combination.[3] As leisure, volunteers carry out tasks delegated to them by certain superiors who are gainfully employed in the organization in which the volunteers serve.

One important difference separating hobbyists from amateurs is that the first lie outside the professional-amateur-public systems of society. Hobbyists are also generally less likely to have a public and they never have professional counterparts (although commercial counterparts may exist). Barbershop singing is a hobby and, incidentally, one that does have a public. Those who pursue this hobby are, as I indicated earlier, activity participants.

Scientifically speaking the proposition that barbershop singing is a profession is untenable, for the art fails to meet the criteria of a profession as defined by many sociologists.[4] A handful of quartets, notably the Buffalo Bills, who appeared in Meredith Willson's *The Music Man* and the Dapper Dans at Disney World and Disneyland, have worked full-time for several years but they cannot alone make up a profession. And we saw earlier that paid quartets were performing in the late nineteenth and early twentieth centuries. Still, over 99 per cent of barbershop singers pursue their art as serious leisure, even though the leading quartets are highly polished and entertaining and good enough to command substantial fees at singouts or perform as headliners at barbershop conventions (both levels). Indeed, the top quartets and choruses are said by barbershop singers to be of professional quality; lacking a true profession and hence a true professional standard against which to measure all performances, this is in reality an empty claim.

The Barbershop Career

Careers can be found in serious leisure just as they can in work and in other major life identities. That is, in each form of serious leisure a distinctive set of background factors and conditions affects the ways novices get launched there. And as is true for all careers, we find in serious leisure careers special contingencies, or chance encounters and events, that work to push leisure practitioners towards different kinds of involvements. In addition these practitioners come upon various turning points, those new directions taken in the leisure career, which are influenced significantly less by chance than by personal effort. Finally, the motivational component associated with all this cannot be ignored. It will be treated in this chapter under the headings of thrills and disappointments in barbershop singing and in the next chapter as part of the analysis of the costs and rewards found there. Missing in most serious leisure careers are the crisp career stages so familiar in the world of work. Still continuity and movement, the essence of any career, are assured in the patterns of contingencies and turning points that serious leisure practitioners invariably pass through.

Background

Many of the men and women sampled had only a dim awareness of barbershop prior to their first direct contact with it. Their image of the art was typically one of quartets, perhaps one shaped by watching *The Music Man.* Often the precontact image was neutral, and for some people even unflattering. As a consequence very few respondents said that they made the first move in the string of events leading them to join a barbershop chapter. Usually an active barbershop singer invited the respondent to an annual show or a weekly choral rehearsal (although never to a quartet rehearsal). This chance meeting between prospective singer and chapter member is the first contingency in the barbershop career.

Approximately two-thirds of the men and women sampled were encouraged by a barbershop friend or acquaintance to attend a show or a rehearsal. This pattern is probably not unique to Calgary, since many of the respondents were living elsewhere in Canada at the time. And, although this study may turn out to be exceptional in this connection, relatives were found to play but a small role in the recruitment process; only four men were invited by a relative, whereas no women were.[5] One man and four women sought out the local chapter on their own, either by making inquiries in their church choirs or by responding to a newspaper notice about the group.

The large majority of both samples was motivated by a special 'leisure lack': an insufficient opportunity to sing choral music.[6] For a minority of this group this lack was total; no singing opportunities whatsoever were available. At the time of contact, however, most respondents were singing in church choirs, where they had developed a craving for more and sometimes better singing outlets. These singers hoped to find in the barbershop chorus what many a barbershop veteran already knows; namely, that such a chorus is likely to be more demanding and therefore of higher musical quality than any number of church choirs.

Despite the motivational push created by the special lack of choral leisure, only half of each sample joined the local chapter within a month or two of initial contact. A shortage of time for the new leisure was the most common reason for this delay, which sometimes lasted several years. These respondents had children to raise or demanding employment. Still, their wish to join the world of close harmony was clearly not frustrated by competing leisure interests. Moreover, a few of those who failed to take up the art more or less on the spot left the community where the initial exposure took place shortly after initial contact. Or they were exposed to barbershop outside the community in which they lived and had no access to it near home.

The finding that relatives played a small role in bringing the men and women of this study into the social world of barbershop can be explained in part by another finding: few relatives were themselves former or current barbershop singers. Only six of the thirty-two respondents reported being encouraged by a relative who was in barbershop (four men, two women). A couple of other respondents said that they subsequently discovered barbershop singers in their extended families, revelations that were triggered by talk about their own involvement. On the whole, however, the families of the respondents were unmusical. It was rare for their parents or siblings to seriously sing or play a musical instrument.

Still this was hardly true for the respondents themselves. Two-thirds of each sample were singing or had sung in a church choir. The women in particular pursued other kinds of musical involvements, often starting as far back as childhood. Nine of them, compared with three men, had been in high school glee clubs. Four women had taken voice lessons and seven had taken lessons on a musical instrument. By contrast no man had received voice lessons and only three had studied on a musical instrument. Thus it is hardly surprising that twice as many women as men (ten compared with five) said they could read music well enough to learn new barbershop songs by this means.

The 1994 Dieringer study of the members of fifty-nine randomly sampled Canadian and American chapters failed to corroborate these findings on two accounts.[7] The Dieringer consultants found that 56 per cent of the sample had played musical instruments and 64 per cent had sung in a school choir before they joined SPEBSQSA. Otherwise the Calgary and Dieringer studies reveal the same patterns of past musical experience. Unfortunately, the second never asked their respondents whether they could read choral music.

It is noteworthy that only one member of each sample had sung in a community chorus. To the extent that such groups sing classical music, they may hold little appeal for the typical barbershop singer, who obviously likes lighter fare. But the widespread inability to read music also prevents him or her from joining a community chorus. To be able to read music is an advantage, insofar as it helps a singer learn a part quickly or sing that part immediately upon encountering it as new music. Yet ear singing, which amounts to learning a part by hearing it sung repeatedly, and 'woodshedding,' or improvising, are traditions in barbershop, although the second is rare among women. Barbershop got its start among men who liked to sing but whose vocal talent was typically undeveloped. They had untrained voices and they could not read music. Yet the music was also simple enough harmonically to allow woodshedding by those providing the harmony parts. The growing emphasis on learning standardized parts has tended in recent decades to make this practice less and less fashionable.[8]

Getting Involved

In addition to attending chorus rehearsals and singing in shows, contests, and singouts, which is the minimal level of participation, newly recruited barbershoppers have three additional opportunities open to them: joining or forming a quartet, developing as a singer, and performing service work. The first two are typical of hobbies everywhere; they offer an opportunity to pursue a substantial self-actualizing and self-expressive personal interest. The third, by contrast, calls on the altruistic spirit of the barbershopper to serve his or her art as a volunteer.

Turning first to the prospect of joining or forming a quartet, I found that most respondents, although somewhat more women (twelve) than men (nine), developed an interest in this aspect of barbershop only after they had joined a chapter. Five men, however, had quartet singing in mind when they went as guests to their first rehearsal. For those whose fascination with quartet singing came later, this new orientation took anywhere from one to twenty years to germinate. Still, most of the respondents who were interested in 'quarteting' were recruited to a quartet or formed one of their own within three to five years of entering the world of barbershop.

Getting involved in a quartet is in many ways an imprecise undertaking. Because each singer is highly exposed here (no one else has the same part), many respondents spoke of an initial lack of confidence in their ability to perform this kind of music. Some accepted invitations to join a quartet only with reluctance. Others experimented with quartet singing by attending jam-session-like evenings with friends. A few of the men acquired a taste for it at one of the novice quartet nights arranged from time to time by the chapter. During these occasions anyone can organize a quartet for the purpose of performing a tune or two before an audience of fellow chapter members.

Even after the singer has become committed to the idea of quartet singing, implementing the decision is usually to some degree problematic. It is a challenge to find four men or women who are willing to devote an additional four hours a week to rehearsing (beyond rehearsing with the chorus), whose voices have an acceptable blend, who can get along with each other, and who can agree on goals for the group, to mention but a few of the possible obstacles. Being recruited to an established quartet often skirts these problems but opens the singer up to others. Established quartets may lose members through transfers at work, surges in occupational or domestic responsibility, changes in leisure interests, or pressure from a spouse who feels the singer is devoting too much time to his or her hobby. In short, quartet singing is always a struggle of one sort or another, which, as I indicate in the next chapter, is nevertheless seen as well worth the effort. It is no wonder that only 21.4 per cent of the Dieringer sample reported singing both in the chapter chorus and in an affiliated quartet.[9]

Self-actualization and self-expression are two of the many rewards to be gained from quartet singing. But they are possibly most strongly felt when gained through a formal program of singing development conducted on the choral level. This occurs in many different ways, only the main ones of which are discussed here. For the women it was possible to receive short sessions of personal vocal instruction (PVI). Here a more or less untrained singer is tutored by a comparatively well-trained member of the same chorus in the art and technique of barbershop (e.g., posture, breath management, tuning of harmonies, matching of vowel sounds) as well as perhaps in how to sing the songs on which the chorus is currently working. At present, the men in this study have no equivalent of PVI. Still, Mel Knight, Director of Music Education and Services for SPEBSQSA, notes that PVI is available in some men's groups but that, in his experience, it is a relatively uncommon service for both sexes.[10] Additionally, the newsletters of both societies carry the occasional article dealing with singing technique and related articles on choral management.

Prior to their annual shows and contests, both the men and the women hold a weekend workshop or two to improve the critical aspects of choral performance. These events are invariably led by a specialist or two, by well-known and experienced coaches from SPEBSQSA or the Sweet Adelines International, or by equally respected members of the chapter. The aspects worked on over the two days are many and varied, among them harmony, pronunciation of lyrics, dynamics (transitions from loud to soft and vice versa), and balance of melodic and harmonic lines.[11] An important consideration in these sessions is 'stage presence' (in men's groups) or 'choreography' (in women's groups) – the facial and bodily gestures and movements designed to enhance the presentation and meaning of the song being sung. Frowning, smiling, raising the arms, and shifting position on the risers are examples. Members of the front line of a chorus may leave their places on the risers to do unison manoeuvres on the stage floor. An event may be enacted there, such as pitching a baseball to a batter and catcher (complete with props) to embellish the chorus's rendition of 'Take Me Out to the Ball Game.'

Further, the Sweet Adelines mix the goals of PVI and the workshops in their regional retreats, held primarily to improve the singing capacity of those in attendance. In this instance improving the annual show or regional contest is not the goal, for singers come to the retreat from different chapters in the area. Instruction is collective and organized around one or more visiting experts. The nearest equivalent available to the Calgary men is for them to attend Harmony College (see chapter 2). In addition, instruction is sometimes available for SPEBSQSA members in district training sessions.

The three kinds of self-improvement on the choral level (PVIs, workshops, and retreats) are also found in a sense on the quartet level, although only among those singers in serious-minded groups. The quartets intending to compete in contests or perform at singouts and annual shows are always striving to better themselves. The mere act of singing on a weekly basis in such an ensemble brings a certain rate of improvement. Moreover the group is likely to have a coach, a local male or female singing expert (to coach quartets of either sex) whose job is to counsel them in such musically difficult areas as balance, harmony, and pronunciation. Since choreography and stage presence are also important in quartet singing, the coach may be asked to advise on these as well.

Finally, the choruses and quartets competing at regional and district contests receive evaluations from panels of judges. The judges are meticulously trained by their respective societies to evaluate one of four dimensions of barbershop singing. Although the societies sometimes use different names to identify the dimensions, they still refer to the same phenomena: the musical arrangement of the song, the vocal production of the song (e.g., balance, harmony, quality, intonation), the interpretation given the song, and the showmanship, or stage presence, with which the song is presented. The judges' comments are widely respected. They can thus serve as a basis for personal and group improvement.

Service work, the third major way of becoming further involved after joining a chorus, is clearly more altruistic than the first two ways, i.e., joining a quartet and developing as a singer. Volunteer help is always welcome and the appeal for it comes from all organizational levels. Regional, district, areal, and international duties need to be fulfilled, including representing one's chapter at the next level, administering business there, and becoming certified as a judge. Would-be volunteers can also choose from a number of informal tasks, such as setting up risers, coordinating social activities, picking up visiting coaches and quartets at the airport, and preparing audiotapes of song parts as learning aids for one's barbershop colleagues.

The service component of the barbershop career tends to begin within the first two to three years of entering the chapter. Perhaps it would be possible to delay this turning point still further but many newcomers are eager to gain acceptance and learn from the inside how the chapter functions. All but a handful of respondents said their service involvement (formal and informal) was either moderate or heavy. That is, at a minimum they sat on a major committee or worked on a major assignment equal in time to attending a second rehearsal each week. Quartet members were as active in this regard as choral members with no quartet interests. Family obligations or work obligations or both sometimes restricted the amount of service a singer could offer, but the expectation that all would help in this area was strongly felt by every respondent.

A singer's artistic development is part of his or her subjective career in barbershop, inasmuch as he or she can discern growing improvement and involvement over the years.[12] Service work finds its place in the subjective barbershop career as one of its turning points and as a road leading to still another area of the social world of barbershop singing. With it comes a feeling of belonging and an opportunity for sociability with like-minded avocational enthusiasts.

Devotees and Participants

The involvement in singing, service work, and artistic improvement is far from uniform, however. Some barbershoppers are clearly more immersed in their serious leisure than others. In barbershop, as in the amateur-professional pursuits I have studied, practitioners can be classified as either participants or devotees. And likewise for this hobby; the devotees are highly dedicated to the art, whereas the participants are only moderately dedicated, but significantly more so than players or dabblers in it.

The sampling procedure used in this study lent itself poorly to any attempt to estimate the proportions of devotees and participants in the Calgary chapters. The decision to draw equal samples of quartet and choral singers gave more numerical weight in those samples to the former than they really have in a typical barbershop chapter. Therefore I can only indicate the lines along which devotees and participants can be distinguished in the art. Most of the main dimensions for doing so have already been introduced; they are service work, individual practice at home, choral and quartet singing (shows, contests, singouts, rehearsals), and singing development (workshops, retreats, PVI, Harmony College).

In my earlier studies of amateurs, the participants have tended to be those who are more or less steadily involved in all the core and at least some of the peripheral activities of the pursuit, as measured by its prevailing standards of involvement. In barbershop, the participants are those who attend most choral rehearsals and sessions for vocal and choral development, sing in the annual show, and go each year to the regional or district contest and convention. Participants here also shoulder a moderate service load.

Devotees are likely to attend somewhat more faithfully the choral rehearsals and developmental sessions and are substantially more likely to be in a busy quartet or be highly active in service work or both. For the men, attending Harmony College is sufficient to win for them at this point in their serious leisure career the label of devotee (because of the time and financial commitment this entails). Devotees spend considerably more than the average amount of time at home practising their singing in general and learning their parts in particular. Participants are inclined to do significantly less of this.

At the lower end of the involvement scale the participant hobbyist shades off into the nonhobbyist category of dabbler, or player. Dabblers play around at barbershop, treating it as casual rather than as serious leisure; they have a poor record of rehearsal attendance and fail to learn their parts. Serious-minded chapters try to rid themselves of these members, who may leave the chapter of their own accord, however, when they sense how much more is expected of them than they are prepared to give. All the Calgary chapters have rules about attending choral rehearsals; unless extenuating circumstances intervene low attendance leads to the cancellation of membership. The pressure to attend reaches its high point four to five rehearsals before a contest or annual show and remains there until the event has passed.

Fortunately, the 1994 Dieringer study contains findings that complement those of the Calgary study. Their survey data revealed several different types of personalities and their distribution in male barbershop singing in North America. Two of these – the 'competitors' and the 'leaders' – seem to correspond to the intense level of involvement of the devotees. They constituted approximately 45 per cent of the Dieringer sample. The 'achieving hobbyists,' or the men 'who want to sing and improve their singing, but are not interested in competing,' are similar to the participants.[13] They made up nearly 20 per cent of the sample. The rest (35 per cent) included the 'affiliators,' or those 'who want to follow and enjoy and like to socialize,' and the 'tag-alongs,' the two groups being the equivalent of dabblers.

Career High Points

Each respondent was asked to identify the thrills, or high points, in his or her barbershop career. These events are important because they motivate the singer to stick with the art in the hope of finding similar experiences again, they demonstrate that diligence and commitment can pay off, and they serve as major turning points in the leisure career. Chance inevitably plays a role in the outcome of thrilling events. But when I describe such an event by saying that it is a high point rather than a career contingency, it is because the barbershopper involved has had a significant degree of control over it. This is evident in the following high points listed by the respondents. They were the same for both sexes.

By far the most important high point, as measured in terms of frequency of mention in the interviews, was competing or winning as a chorus or quartet in a regional, district, areal, or international contest. As an experience, this high point refers to being swallowed up in a sea of barbershop song, in a sea of pure, ringing, consonant harmonies to which the audience responds with avid appreciation. These conditions – the production of the song and its reception – are most commonly joined at contests, where chorus members are most likely to concentrate to the fullest, inspired as they are by the possibility of winning or at least placing well.

No other high point discussed in the interviews came close to this one in terms of personal impact and frequency of mention. Singing to any appreciative audience (not just the ones at the contests) and performing singouts as a quartet were tied as the second most prominent thrill. It is safe to conclude that singing well before any 'good' audience – which is one enamoured of the music – is what barbershop singers come to live for in their serious leisure. A female respondent described her first experience onstage at the regional chorus contest:

> I couldn't believe how I felt as we began to sing 'Sweet Georgia Brown' in that big hall. I could see the audience starting to move with the rhythm as we sang through the first chorus. And I felt like all 65 of our voices were one big voice, which was my own and that the audience was part of us as well. I was a mass of goose bumps by the time we finished the tune. The audience's reaction was just terrific.

The disappointments found in barbershop indirectly tell us something about its high points. The women much more than the men (ten respondents to four) listed as their first and often sole disappointment an unexpectedly low placement in a contest, as gauged by the goals the group had set for itself. It is a thrill to sing in contests, but one of the risks incurred in pursuing this thrill is failure, in this case low placement. And it is quite possible at both the chorus and the quartet levels to sing well but place in the middle of the list of contestants, for competition is intense at the regional and district conventions and even more so at 'international.'

A quarter of each sample described as disappointing the low commitment of certain members of the chapter who, in our terms, are borderline or possibly even full-fledged dabblers. About the same percentage of men found disappointing a recent decision by some of the best singers in the chapter to leave it to form another chorus composed more exclusively of high-quality voices. This is the splinter group mentioned earlier. Although men's and women's barbershop choruses operating in other cities have experienced similar schisms and accompanying disappointment, this is hardly a routine occurrence. Nonetheless, tension lurks in many a chorus between those who feel anyone who likes to sing and can carry a tune should be admitted (this is the official policy of the three societies) and those who feel their chorus should be composed strictly of singers who know their art well. All in all, however, the disappointments add up to no more than a minor countersentiment to the high points so mightily cherished by those in this study. As explained further in the next chapter the sweet in barbershop far outweighs the bitter.

Ending the Career

Since this study examined only currently involved singers, I lack systematic data on how the barbershop career comes to an end. Discussion with singers of both sexes suggests, however, that a proper investigation of the matter will likely uncover at least four reasons for leaving the hobby: outside commitments, physical problems or death, loss of interest, and disenchantment. A barbershopper might also drop out for a combination of these.

Outside commitments, such as those demanded by home and work, temporarily sidelined some of the respondents and prevented a number of others from participating to the extent they would have liked. Commitments of this sort can also remove a singer permanently from the barbershop scene as, for example, in a job transfer to another city.[14] A growing small business, a coveted promotion to a more responsible and time-consuming position, or an increase in pressure from one's spouse or children to stay home more often are among the typical outside commitments said in barbershop circles to pull a significant number of its enthusiasts from the art for several years, if not permanently.

Death as the reason for ending the career indicates that singers can and often do stay in barbershop well into old age. For some, the long hours on the risers become too painful or too exhausting, forcing them to accept an exclusive diet of service work or to sit at the side of the chorus during rehearsals and performances. It is not unusual to see one or two elderly men or women seated, perhaps in wheelchairs, at one end of the risers while they and their chorus perform. Their voices are still good but their physical condition necessitates this special arrangement. But despite these accommodations, infirmity and immobility do eventually force some singers to resign from the chapter as active members.

> First went the chorus singing (my choice) because of spinal-stenosis-induced leg problems. Then went my quartet singing (definitely *not* my choice) because of stroke-induced speech problems in 1991. Before that, barbershop singing had been my favorite hobby, but I didn't know how much it meant to me until I could no longer participate.[15]

Fortunately for this man, a speech program eventually restored his capacity to sing with his quartet.

Disenchantment contributes significantly to the loss of interest in barbershop and may enhance indirectly the appeal of another serious leisure field. Disenchantment can result in specialization, in a shift to quartet singing only. Or it may simply push the singer out of four-part harmony into the sprawling domain of aimless casual leisure.

The disappointments mentioned earlier are not generally disenchanting. Rather disenchantments spring from situations that a barbershopper has little or no control over and that generate a sense of desperation the only apparent solution to which is to leave the chapter. Among the sources of disenchantment are expenses, cliquishness, objectionable policies (e.g., tolerance of mediocrity, insistence on high standards), lack of leadership, weak or otherwise insufferable directors, and a preference for another style of unaccompanied, four-part harmony.

It appears that most barbershop chapters strive mightily to moderate the costs of this leisure. They conduct fund-raising campaigns and widely promote the sale of tickets to their shows. Even then, dues, trips to conventions, and uniforms and costumes take a considerable financial toll on members, especially the new ones, who must initially pay a substantial amount towards the uniforms and costumes used by their chorus.

Conclusions

All barbershop singers are initially attracted to their hobby by the self-interested goal of personal musical expression and many are also attracted by the possibility of personal musical development. Somewhat later a substantial number of them gain additional enjoyment from the altruistic activities involved in the organization and administration of the art. As they pursue these goals they find themselves drawn into a profound serious leisure career embedded in an engaging social world of song and friendship. Here as elsewhere in serious leisure, career advancement along the lines of accumulated skill, knowledge, and experience is a powerful motivator. This sort of personal development and expression motivates people because it is so extraordinarily rewarding. Still, it does take some time before the neophyte in barbershop discovers the rewards it has to offer.

This is true in part because, as we have already seen, it occasionally rains in the usually sun-swept land of barbershop song. In other words, enthusiasts of the art must occasionally endure certain costs, costs that seem to contrast sharply with the many rewards they find there. These dark days serve as tests. Such days also bring to light the enigma of why anyone would willingly endure in his or her leisure even one poignant cost. Is this not what leisure is all about – avoiding the pains of the disagreeable while taking up the hunt for the pleasurable? The presence of costs in the hobby of barbershop raises at least two questions. Why sing this music seriously and, more particularly, why sing it competitively?

CHAPTER FIVE

Why Sing?

Sir William Osler at a farewell dinner in 1905 said:

> No man is really happy or safe without a hobby, and it makes precious little difference what the outside interest may be – botany, beetles or butterflies, roses, tulips or irises; fishing, mountaineering or antiquities – anything will do so long as he straddles a hobby and rides it hard.

Hobbies are a good thing it seems. Yet, one apparently contradictory side of serious leisure, given the culturally dominant belief that all leisure is casual activity, is the paradox that those who engage in it encounter costs *and* rewards, both of which can be sharply felt.[1] It is precisely this contradiction – realizing important values in the face of adversity – that speaks most directly and consistently to the motivational question of why some people take up forms of leisure at which they 'must work.'

So poignant are the costs of serious leisure that many practitioners ask themselves from time to time why they do it. This means that researchers in this area must always consider such costs in any analysis of the 'durable benefits' of serious leisure, which constitute one of the six qualities that define it. The costs offset the durable benefits to some extent, while combining with them to form patterns of costs and rewards unique to each pursuit. Further research may allow us to generalize these patterns in certain ways. For the present, however, one effective way to explore them in a given amateur, hobbyist, or career volunteer field is from the perspective provided by the following simple proposition taken from social exchange theory. The main costs and rewards of an activity, when psychologically weighed against each other, result in a personal sense of 'profit' or 'loss.'[2] This was the model used to examine the costs and rewards experienced by the barbershop singers of Calgary.[3]

If we want to know what motivates barbershop singers to pursue their hobby despite certain costs, we must go to their everyday world for the most detailed and informative answer to this question. In this respect hobbyists appear to be similar to amateurs. My research on amateurs demonstrates that the costs and rewards that they experience and talk about are highly specific to each amateur pursuit. This 'folk,' or everyday, understanding of these costs and rewards cannot be predicted from the various overarching propositions about the broad benefits of leisure. For this reason it is important to proceed from the assumption that hobbyists, too, have typical but distinct patterns of costs and rewards. One major task of the Calgary study was to discover this pattern for barbershop singing.

Rewards

The rewards of a pursuit are the more or less routine values that attract and hold its practitioners and are to be distinguished from its thrills, which will be covered in the next section. Working from a list of nine possible rewards, the respondents were asked to select those that applied to them and then to rank their selections from most to least rewarding. I had developed this list inductively in the course of my eight earlier studies of amateurs and professionals. It is of note that some of these rewards (e.g., self-actualization) are recognizable as generalized benefits from the social psychology of leisure. Here, however, these rewards were also used as probes to generate discussion on the ways in which each reward is more particularly expressed in the leisure pursuit under study.

A file card with the following list was presented to each singer:

1. Personal enrichment (cherished experiences, including exceptional audience rapport)
2. Self-actualization (developing skills and abilities)

3. Self-expression (expressing skills and abilities already developed)
4. Self-image (known to others as a barbershop singer)
5. Enjoyable, fun (senses of play, hedonistic pleasure)
6. Re-create oneself, regenerate oneself through the hobby after a day's work
7. Social attraction (associating with other barbershop singers)
8. Group accomplishment (group effort in producing good music, a good show)
9. Financial return (from the hobby)

After the rewards and their ranking were discussed at length with each respondent, he or she was encouraged, in line with the exploratory mission of the study, to add other rewards to the list. No additions were suggested, however.

Each respondent's ranking of the rewards was weighted according to the ranking given then. The weights were then summed up for each reward for the male and female samples. The totals are presented in parentheses in Table 1. The rank of each reward, as determined by this procedure, is expressed by the number to the left of the parentheses.

TABLE 1
Weighted Selection of Rewards by Rank of Choice

	Rank (total) of respondents' weights	
Reward	Men	Women
Personal enrichment	1 (133)	1 (124)
Self-actualization	3 (103)	3 (110)
Self-expression	6 (81)	5 (82)
Self-image	8 (62)	6 (60)
Enjoyable, fun	2 (113)	2 (118)
Re-create oneself	7 (64)	8 (48)
Social attraction	5 (82)	6 (60)
Group accomplishment	4 (97)	4 (91)
Financial return	9 (7)	9 (8)

Although a larger sample and a more precise measurement of rewards might have produced larger differences between men and women, the ones found here were too small to be significant at this exploratory stage of research on barbershop singing. Likewise, no significant differences could be observed in the reward patterns of choral and quartet singers. But the small subsamples indicate that we should treat these findings with caution. These limitations aside, however, there are certain clear rewards to be gained from performing this art.

Personal enrichment is the most powerful reward to be found in barbershop singing. It comes through the experience of performing – mainly in presenting a polished show or selection of songs before an appreciative audience or in competing in regional, district, areal, and national conventions with other quartets or choruses for the honour of the highest or at least one of the highest evaluations by the judges. The respondent's singing unit did not have to win or even place especially well for him or her to define competition of this sort as enriching. As one enthusiastic female quartet singer described it:

> Singing in a quartet gives you all kinds of freedom, a licence to do certain things you can't do in a chorus. You have more freedom to entertain, to sing to the people [in the audience], to sing the songs they know and so on. That's the most important part of barbershopping for me.

One of the men, who limited his singing to the chapter chorus, observed:

> When you're singing, the sound around you is incredible. You feel like you're being carried away with it. It's absolutely inspiring. But, you know, it seems to take a contest or the annual show to bring out the best in us, to get to that level of perfection where the chords ring and you feel like you're being swallowed up by the music itself.

It was evident from the interviews that a newcomer to barbershop is, to a considerable extent, denied all this, the most fundamental reward, until he or she participates in an annual chapter show or regional or district contest. My observations suggest that such participation is a crucial experience, after which members of Sweet Adelines International and SPEBSQSA are substantially less likely to renounce the art because they see more costs than benefits.

The enjoyment of barbershop singing is its second most powerful reward. It is enjoyable to sing one's part well, much as it is enjoyable to play the violin well or skate well. This is a personal reward, which, when done on a social basis, becomes 'fun.'[4] It is both fun and enjoyable to be immersed in the resonance of unaccompanied four-part harmony to which one is a competent contributor as a member of either a quartet or a chorus. Although fun and enjoyment may be found in such casual leisure as chatting in a hot tub with friends or watching a television sitcom with the family, this reward is only possible in barbershop (and other serious leisure) because the practitioner has developed a substantial foundation of skill, knowledge, and experience that is expressed in interaction with others.

Self-actualization – the third most prevalent reward – is especially evident in barbershop singing, a popular art that many neophytes take up with little more than a minimally acceptable level of voice control and ability to hear notes (ear). The local chapter offers training in these areas, which means that those who continue as members eventually enjoy the reward of personal musical development as a singer. Of course, the pace of this development depends on how much the singer puts into it, namely, on how much he or she practises parts and technique and how faithfully he or she attends weekly choral or quartet rehearsals.

Although significant for the respondents, the remaining rewards were nonetheless generally weaker than the three just mentioned. A somewhat larger number of men than women saw group accomplishment as an important reward. The reason for the discrepancy between the two samples is unclear. That group accomplishment is less important as a reward than the individual rewards of personal enrichment, fun and enjoyment, and self-actualization attests the dominant self-interestedness that drives amateur and hobbyist pursuits, contrasted with the more evenly balanced self-interestedness and altruism that leads to career volunteering. The other rewards on the list – self-expression, social attraction, and so on – can be regarded as additional values to be gained from participating in barbershop, although of clearly secondary import. They appear to be too weak to offset alone the costs of the hobby or the appeal of alternative leisure, be it serious or casual.

The relatively low rank given the reward of social attraction begs further discussion, given the emphasis that male barbershop singers in particular place on camaraderie. I frequently heard during both the interviews and the periods of observation that there is considerable friendliness and good-fellowship in barbershop circles (notwithstanding certain social costs discussed later in this chapter). Closer examination of this claim indicates, however, that the camaraderie is closely associated with the production of the music itself. That is, barbershoppers feel a strong fellowship – a wave of warmth and friendliness – when they sing together. An important facet of the fun and personal enrichment gained from barbershop singing, then, is its camaraderie.

In short, the social attraction of the art is inextricably tied to its two highest rewards. Further support for this generalization about the relatively low rank of the reward of social attraction comes from the finding that, when asked to identify their close friends, the men found only 20 per cent to be in barbershop. Of the women's close friends, 31 per cent were found here.

Thrills

Thrills, or high points, are the sharply exciting events and occasions that stand out in the minds of those who pursue serious leisure of some sort. In general, they tend to be associated with the rewards of self-enrichment and, to a lesser extent, self-actualization and self-expression.[5] That is, thrills in serious leisure may be seen as situated manifestations of the more abstract rewards; they are what the practitioners in each field seek as concrete expressions of the rewards they find there. They are important because they motivate the participant to stick with the pursuit in the hope of finding similar experiences again and again and because they demonstrate that diligence and commitment can pay off.

Each respondent was asked to identify the thrills in his or her career as a barbershop singer. Here, too, no significant differences between the men and the women could be found: both said that by far the most important thrill was competing or winning as a chorus or quartet in a regional, district, areal, or international contest. As an experience this high point refers to being swallowed up in a sea of barbershop song, surrounded by pure, ringing, consonant harmonies to which the audience avidly responds:

> There is really no way to describe it, I guess. The chords are so big and ringing, and they're all around you as you sing yourself. I feel this especially in the tags, as we are in the process of ending the more dramatic tunes ... At any rate this is what keeps me in barbershop. (female singer with seven years of experience in barbershop)

These conditions – the production of the song and its reception – are most commonly joined at contests, where members of choruses and quartets are most likely to concentrate to their fullest, motivated by the possibility of placing among the top three or four contestants.

No other thrill discussed in the interviews came close to this one in terms of personal impact and frequency of mention. Singing to any appreciative audience (not just one at a contest) and performing publicly in a quartet were tied as the second most prominent thrills. It is certainly possible to conclude that singing well and doing so before a 'good audience' – in other words, one that likes the music and shows it – is what barbershop singers come to live for in their serious leisure.

Psychologically, this thrill meets the criteria for being a 'flow experience,' which is one of the main generalized benefits discussed in the literature on the social psychology of leisure.[6] But, getting down to the level of everyday life, how does performing barbershop before a receptive audience actually generate flow?

Csikszentmihalyi identified several characteristics of this psychological process. Applied to barbershop, performance merges the action of singing with one's awareness of it to form a single sensation. Further, performance centres attention exclusively on the limited stimulus field of making music. Especially in choral singing the practitioner loses his or her sense of ego, or self, by becoming enveloped in the process of musical production. Arising from all this is the feeling of competence as a singer. Moreover, the individual singer's goal at this point – which is to sing his or her part as well as possible – is unambiguous, whereas feedback as to how well that goal is met is immediately and directly evident in the response of the audience to the music. The flow experience impresses on the practitioner the autotelic nature of barbershop singing; it is an activity that is intensely rewarding in and of itself.

Costs

The various studies of amateurs revealed three kinds of costs associated with such pursuits: tensions, dislikes, and disappointments.[7] This, the first study of hobbyists in this regard, suggests that they, too, endure similar experiences. Let us turn to the disappointments.

Disappointments

We saw in the preceding chapter that disappointments combine with thrills to help give substance to the barbershop career. Here we examine the same disappointments from a motivational perspective, as one of the costs offsetting the rewards of barbershop. It was pointed out earlier that more women than men listed as their first and often sole disappointment an unexpectedly low placement in a contest as measured against their group's goals. It is a thrill to sing in contests, but one risk in pursuing this thrill is to fail; that is, to receive a low placement.

A quarter of each sample described as disappointing the low commitment of certain members of their chapters, who are, sociologically speaking, borderline or full-fledged dabblers rather than genuine hobbyists.[8] Low commitment may even be evident at the singouts:

> It's really disappointing when you have a singout planned for the chorus and you have to cancel it because not enough members turn out for it. It's the lack of commitment that gets me. (male singer with two years of experience in barbershop)

We also noted earlier that about 25 per cent of the men described as disappointing a recent decision by some of the best singers in their chapter to leave it to form the splinter group composed of more uniformly high-quality voices. Although there are men's and women's barbershop choruses in other cities that have known similar schisms and accompanying disappointment, this is hardly a routine occurrence anywhere.

Dislikes

When I asked the interviewees to identify and discuss what they disliked about barbershop, I indicated that I was interested in more profound matters than pet peeves. I see dislikes as problems requiring a person to make significant adjustments, including possibly even leaving the leisure pursuit. As was the case in my research on amateurs, dislikes in the hobby of barbershop were highly specific to the art itself.

Although only two men and two women said they had no dislikes whatsoever, there was a lack of widespread agreement on particular dislikes. About half the men said they disliked the absence of leadership that has affected their chapter at times, and about half said they disliked the low commitment of some members (defined earlier as a disappointment by other respondents). The sentiment about leadership is an indictment against certain choral directors who were seen as incapable of controlling extraneous talk during rehearsals, persuading members to practise their parts, or effecting improvement in the chorus. Weak leadership can lead the best members of the chapter to leave – perhaps to form a new chapter or seek another singing outlet. It may also encourage new recruits to ook elsewhere for their leisure.

Low commitment is often manifested in a failure to learn one's part sufficiently, in spotty attendance at rehearsals, and in persistent problems with basic singing technique. The quality of the chorus is undermined by such deficiencies, as is the enjoyment of those who strive for excellence as a principal reward of their leisure. These deficiencies also absorb precious rehearsal time:

> I dislike the pace of the chorus – they're too slow at learning [the

> songs] and getting it all into performing shape. It seems like we work on the same stuff all the time, going over it and over it again and again. (male singer with ten years of barbershop experience)

As for the more weakly committed members, many of them find considerable reward in the heady experience of presenting a show or competing in a contest, although they find scant reward in self-actualization. Thus, they start coming regularly to rehearsals only a month or so before one of these events, when attendance becomes mandatory for those who want to participate in them.

The women disliked the presence of poorly committed members almost as much as the men. As strong a dislike among the women, however, was the 'politics' of barbershop. Politics in barbershop, as in many amateur pursuits, centres on the use and acquisition of power.[9] Respondents noted power struggles over the selection of new directors, some wanting proper taskmistresses, others wanting less demanding leaders. Likewise, politics was said to spring up for similar reasons around the election of chapter presidents. Among the side effects of these struggles was the reluctance of some members to become involved in the administrative affairs of the group and the attendant atmosphere of hostility that drives away newcomers and, for that matter, some veterans whose patience has run its course. But possibly the most unsettling aspect of chapter politics is its tendency to stymie the overall development of the chorus.

Other dislikes were mentioned only infrequently. Although respondents of both sexes noted the existence of cliques in their chapters, only a few felt strongly enough about them to classify them as a dislike. Cliques do seem to be inevitable in barbershop to some extent since the members of the quartets within a chorus tend to hang around together, as do smokers, who nowadays are ostracized during rehearsal breaks. Likewise, a number of men mentioned the presence of politics, but few of them called it a dislike. A small number of women (three) disliked the complaining and backbiting of certain members. In the final analysis, however, the dislikes amount to little more than minor sentiments in the leisure lives of these barbershop singers, something that many respondents were quick to point out.

Tensions

Compared with such amateur performance fields as theatre, instrumental music, and stand-up comedy, the hobby of barbershop singing is relatively free of tensions, particularly the one of stage fright. Stage fright is an emotional state that arises in connection with a person's problem of sustaining an identity in the face of apprehensiveness about his or her capacity to do so. It develops when performers know in advance that their performance could bring scrutiny from others in response to a slip, flaw, or failure.[10]

Approximately half of each sample said they suffered mild nervousness before every performance or suffered it before especially important performances such as those given in contests. Some quartet members said they become nervous when singing in front of other barbershopppers, since they can be a highly critical audience. To some extent, stage fright is related to the degree of personal exposure to the public; it is more likely to develop in quartet singing than in choral singing, in solo work than in ensemble work. It is also a tension that is more common among novice singers than among veterans, the latter having grown accustomed to performing before audiences.

But even more common as a preperformance sentiment is what I referred to in a study of amateur theatre as 'eager anticipation': performers who are prepared, and thus confident of their capacity to present their part well, are eager to go onstage to show the audience what they can do.[11] Instead of being fearful of and hence repelled by the prospect of public scrutiny, they are attracted to it for the approbation that is potentially there. Overall, a somewhat larger percentage of barbershop singers experienced this emotion than the one of stage fright.

A more diffuse but nevertheless universal tension in barbershop is the one that has developed around the question of whether everyone who likes to sing and can carry a tune should be admitted to the chorus (the official policy of the international barbershop societies) or whether the chorus should be strictly composed of singers who know their art well. I heard considerable informal, and sometimes formal, discussion of this matter in the four chapters that were studied. The same tension plagues amateur fine arts groups and there, as in barbershop, it is rarely alleviated to everyone's satisfaction. Rather, my observations in barbershop and the amateur performing arts suggest that most of the more able and committed practitioners tolerate those who are less able and committed because certain minimum numbers of performers are needed to carry out different kinds of music, theatre, dance, and the like. In barbershop, for example, relatively weak singers are often seen (usually grudgingly) as better than no singers at all. An insufficient number of voices would mean that the able and committed would be left with no outlet whatsoever for their musical aspirations.

Conclusions

I have been pursuing two major aims in this chapter: to further develop my inductive theory of barbershop singing and to explore the ratio of costs and rewards experienced there. The two are closely related so far as this aspect of the overall study is concerned. Turning first to the theory, we now have a set of detailed, partially interrelated generalizations about the specific rewards (including thrills) and costs (including dislikes, disappointments, and tensions) and their interconnnections as these bear on the decision to enter and remain in the social world of barbershop. These generalizations also describe some of the most significant everyday life experiences found in barbershop.

On the subject of the ratio of costs and rewards, we may note that, notwithstanding the conceptual efforts of George Homans and other social exchange theorists, no calculus exists in social psychology by which we might compute for barbershop an 'attraction quotient' of rewards over costs. Yet I am convinced from my observations and interviews that these singers derive a substantial 'profit' in values from their serious leisure as they weigh its costs against its rewards. It works something like this. When Shirley Trudel joined the Chair City Pipers chapter of Harmony, Incorporated she had to face the costs of learning the specialized language of barbershop singing, which were, however, eventually overridden by her love for the music.

Barber Shop-Talk

Being a new barbershopper is very confusing,
I don't understand all the words they're using,
I learned the songs we were taught to sing
Then they asked me if I heard a 'chord ring'!

I ducked when the basses were told to 'swipe,'
And really struck out when they threw in 'pitch pipe.'
'From the edge' means nothing to me,
And whose initials are 'H.J.T.P.?'

Someone please tell me, where is 'up on risers'
Before I'm dealt any more surprises.
And where should I go to 'back off on the tag?'
In learning these phrases I seem to lag.

But there is one word I'm not forgetting.
What do they mean when they say 'woodshedding?'
I love this hobby and I love to sing. Oh –
but, please, won't someone teach me the 'lingo.'
(from 'Introducing Harmony, Inc.' pamphlet, n.d.)

The profit of excess reward over cost is highly attractive. But, although it was found that the rewards and thrills psychologically, if not numerically, surpass the disappointments, dislikes, and tensions, the way of measuring profit used up to this point is tautological. Fortunately, profit can also be measured in other ways. For example, I asked each interviewee to talk about his or her future plans in barbershop. One woman was on the verge of quitting, disenchanted with the quality of the local chapter, and one man said that, at age seventy-five, it was soon time to retire. But they were the exceptions. Eleven men and three women discussed the ways they hoped to expand their involvement. The remainder of the two samples said that they had reached a satisfying level of participation, a level at which they intended to stay. Another measure of profit is available in the way in which barbershop singers of both sexes enthusiastically try to recruit members to their chapters and proudly promote the sale of tickets to their annual shows among their friends and acquaintances.

For those people who make it their hobby, barbershop singing is truly and profoundly satisfying leisure. When it is as rewarding, 'due leisure' serves its participants well:

> A day's work is a day's work, neither more nor less, and the man who does it needs a day's sustenance, a night's repose, and due leisure, whether he be painter or ploughman. (George Bernard Shaw, *An Unsocial Socialist,* 1932)

The place of truly and profoundly satisfying due leisure in life brings us to the question of the social marginality of barbershop singing in the larger community.

CHAPTER SIX

Work in Leisure

I have argued over the years that amateurs and the activities they pursue are marginal in society, since amateurs are neither dabblers nor professionals.[1] Several properties of amateurism give substance to this hypothesis. First (as incongruent as it may seem), amateur leisure is characterized by an extensive positive commitment to a pursuit, as measured, for example, by a sizeable investment of time and energy in it.[2] Second, amateurism is pursued with noticeable seriousness (i.e., as a type of serious leisure) with such passion that Erving Goffman once qualified amateurs, among others, as the 'quietly disaffiliated.'[3] Third, amateurism tends to be uncontrollable; it engenders in the practitioner a desire to engage in the activity beyond the time and money available for it. Whereas some casual leisure can be uncontrollable, too, our marginality hypothesis implies that this proclivity is significantly stronger among amateurs. Fourth, amateurs occupy the status of peripheral members of the profession on which they model their activities, while being judged in those activities by the standards of that profession.

Marginality, as the term is used here, is different from the idea of 'marginal man' used by sociologists for many years to describe the lifestyles of immigrants. The latter are marginal because they are typically caught between two cultures in such a way that their marginality becomes a way of life, a condition touching nearly every corner of their existence. Although this ethnic marginality and the leisure marginality on which this chapter focuses are both centred on peripheral and ambiguous social statuses, the second kind of marginality is hardly as pervasive as the first. Rather, leisure marginality is a segmented, or limited, marginality, which accompanies certain uncommon or unusual statuses.[4]

Here, as in ethnic marginality, we find among the status incumbents themselves (as well as in the wider community) an *ambiguity*, or a lack of clarity, as to who these marginal people really are and what they really do. The study of barbershop singers, like the other studies that I have conducted on serious leisure, indicates that this ambiguity has several facets. On its cultural side ambiguity is manifested narrowly as a conflict of expectations and broadly as a conflict of values (e.g., commitment to special interests or rewards).[5] On its relational side, incongruent status arrangements develop, as when amateurs in pursuit of their leisure goals help professionals reach their work goals. Psychologically, practitioners may become ambivalent about their serious leisure when, in the course of trying to integrate their hobby into their everyday lives, they begin to realize just how marginal they are here. In summing up these ideas about ambiguity, then, I am suggesting that all serious leisure, including barbershop singing, is found at the margin of the social institution of leisure.[6] We shall return to this proposition in the concluding section of this chapter.

Marginal statuses are common in industrial societies, where rapid change spawns new kinds of work and leisure. Still, with the passage of time some marginal work and leisure becomes less, even much less, ambiguous. Some may even become central.[7] The present study of barbershop singers suggests, nevertheless, that such a transformation is yet to take place among amateurs and hobbyists.

In my theoretical elaboration of the amateur studies, I raised the possibility of extending the foregoing ideas about marginality to all areas of serious leisure.[8] The observations and interview data reported in this chapter examine that possibility with reference to both the hobby of barbershop singing and the hobbyists themselves. What is the nature of marginality here and what is its extent? The three principal areas of community life in which the marginality of serious leisure manifests itself are the family, the workplace, and, of course, the social institution of leisure. We turn to the first of these.

Family

By way of background for our discussion of marginal leisure and the family, let us look at the amount of time a singer typically devotes to his or her barbershop activities. The main activities were set out in chapter 4: service work for barbershop organizations, individual practice at home, choral and quartet singing (in shows, contests, singouts, rehearsals), and personal singing development (instruction, workshops, retreats). All these activities considered, the men averaged 12 hours per week, the women 9.8 hours. The women practised more on their own, however, putting in an average of 2.4 hours per week compared with 1.1 hours put in by the men.[9]

The term 'family' was used throughout the study as an umbrella concept for all steady adult relationships with a member of the opposite sex, whether children were present and whether the relationships were solemnized in a marriage ceremony. According to this definition, thirteen women said they lived in a family relationship (nine were married), compared with fifteen men (all married). One single man, one widower, and two divorcées rounded out the two subsamples.

I discussed in each interview whether the respondent's partner accepted, tolerated, or rejected the nature and extent of his or her involvement in barbershop. Significant sex differences resulted from this question, although they are belied by some of the interview data. Eleven women and thirteen men said their partners accepted their barbershop activities; the partners directly encouraged the respondents in one way or another to participate in their hobby. The difference here between men and women is minuscule. Moreover, it would be insignificant were it not that four of the women lived with a boyfriend or companion, a kind of relationship where each person typically has less control over the leisure activities of the other than he or she would were they married. Given the centrality of barbershop in the lives of these respondents, it is highly probable that its rejection by the boyfriend or companion would be felt early in the formation of the relationship and seriously hinder, if not completely terminate, its further development.

When recalculated only for the nine married women in the sample, it was found that 33 per cent (three respondents) had husbands who tolerated their barbershop involvements; this compares with 20 per cent (three respondents) of the fifteen married men whose wives had a similar orientation.[10] One of the divorcées also said that her ex-husband's rejection of her hobby was partly to blame for the dissolution of their marriage. Discussions during the interviews and the observation sessions revealed that a number of married female barbershop singers are subject to pressure from their husbands to limit severely, if not entirely, the time they devote to their serious leisure. In some instances singing and rehearsing are accepted, but ventures into chapter service work are seen as going too far. 'Going too far' commonly refers to that point beyond which the husbands believe that either they or the rest of the family or both are being substantially neglected:

> He's not musical. He'll come to the shows alright, but I think he sees it as a duty. He complains a lot when I do work for the Board [of Directors of the chapter] – 'the family needs you here, dinner is always so rushed on rehearsal nights.' You know, that kind of thing. (a singer with twelve years of experience)

> He accepts it [her barbershopping] reluctantly. He never shows any excitement or interest in my experiences there, in how much I get out of it, and things like that. I think he has come to only two annual shows and then out of a sense of duty, I am sure. I know he feels put upon when I rush off on rehearsal night and haven't prepared a full meal for him and the rest of the family. (singer with ten years of experience)

To avoid accusations of neglect, some women go to great lengths to ensure that basic family needs are met before they depart for a barbershop function. Many of those with families told how they prepare in advance all the meals they will miss while away for a weekend convention or chapter retreat. They frequently arrive at these events exhausted from this effort, get little sleep while there, and return home to a pile of dirty dishes and, for some, the prospect of going to work the next day. It is no wonder that they often defined retreats and conventions as 'well-deserved holidays.'

A husband's involvement in his wife's barbershop life is typically less than a wife's involvement in that of her husband. Eleven of the thirteen husbands or partners and the fifteen wives attended some or all of the annual shows put on by the respondent's chapter. But only five husbands or partners routinely went to the afterglows compared with eleven wives. Wives also frequently accompanied their husbands to the yearly chapter banquet, whereas the opposite never occurred since the women's banquet excludes men. Husbands and partners are rare indeed at the regional conventions of the Sweet Adelines International, whereas nearly half the wives go to some or all of SPEBSQSA's district conventions. This difference by the way cannot be traced to the demands of a job, for the conventions are held on weekends and the same proportions of men and women in the subsamples were employed outside the home.

It turns out that a wife's involvement in her husband's barbershop activities can be extremely broad. For example, the women's auxiliary is an old and enduring tradition in the SPEBSQSA. It is common for the members of many of these auxiliaries to busy themselves with such activities as fund-raising, selling tickets for the annual shows, and applying makeup to the men before they go onstage to present those shows. On a more informal level, a barbershop wife might coach her husband's singing, play on the piano the accompanying parts of a song he is trying to learn, or prepare snacks on the evenings when his quartet rehearses in their home.

I have no idea how the wives view this support role since they were never interviewed. What is evident, however, is that married male singers, so far as barbershop is concerned, generally lead less stressful family lives than married female singers. We may conclude therefore that the women much more than the men experience the marginality possible in a serious leisure activity such as barbershop. The marginality is experienced as role and value conflict.

How typical this pattern is of other hobbies remains to be seen. Barbershop is by tradition exclusive. The choruses and quartets at the singouts and annual shows have almost always been composed of one sex or the other and those at the official contests and concerts are invariably composed this way. It follows that in this pursuit a spouse or partner can only rarely, if ever, participate directly with the singer, as is possible in a number of other hobbies, among them, fishing, collecting, cross-country skiing, and, in a similar vein, performing in church choirs.

Work

The male sample was employed in a fair range of occupations running from the skilled trades to the liberal professions. Most of the sample, however, worked in the commerce and small business sectors of the economy. Nine men held high school diplomas and some of them had also earned advanced technical certificates. Five others had earned bachelor's degrees and one a master's degree.[11] Two had never completed high school, even though one of them had gone on to complete a bachelor's degree. Eleven were employed, five were retired. Overall, the sample was unmistakably white-collar and middle-class. Missing were representative numbers of professionals and blue-collar workers. Only two professionals – a geophysicist and an accountant – fell into the sample, which also contained neither upper-level corporate managers nor other organizational executives.

The part of the female sample employed outside the home was entirely white-collar and heavily concentrated in clerical work. Four members of the sample were housewives, ten were employed outside the home (one part-time), one was a certificate student, and one was a widow living on a pension. All had high school diplomas, to which some had also added an advanced technical certificate. One women had earned a bachelor's degree.

I occasionally heard expressions of concern about this occupational concentration in the white-collar range, although it was chiefly the men who voiced them. Barbershop has been struggling in recent decades with the problem of declining numbers. This has led some singers to speculate that new chapter members might be found in other parts of the community.[12] Indeed they might, although we saw in chapter 4 that new members are now recruited almost exclusively through personal channels – through word of mouth circulated among friends, acquaintances, and, more rarely, relatives. This suggests that they usually come from the same social level as existing members, since friendship networks, not to mention family circles, tend to be socioeconomically homogeneous. George Homans observes:

> First, the status of persons in all stratified societies, whether their status is inherited or achieved, is principally determined by their occupations, in the largest sense of the word, and by the incomes their occupations win for them ... Second, the more nearly equal persons are in public status, the more apt they are to interact in the private field, the sphere of leisure, of after working hours, of 'social' interaction: eating together, playing together, going to parties together.[13]

Another possible barrier to recruitment is musical taste. Although traditional barbershop song is simple and of potentially wide appeal, it is nevertheless true that many people dislike it. It was pointed out earlier that even some of the respondents were lukewarm towards barbershop until they had participated in a rehearsal or two or attended an annual show. And some admitted that it is certainly more fun to sing in a chorus or quartet than to listen to either. In any case, a taste bias may be operating here; blue-collar workers, on the one hand, and upper-level managers, executives, and professionals, on the other, generally seem to prefer different types of music, whether as producers or consumers. For example, acid rock and country and western tend to attract the first and jazz and classical music tend to attract the second.

The discussion to this point suggests that, so far as the demographic variable of work is concerned, the hobby of barbershop is anything but marginal. It appeals to a wide, mid-socioeconomic range of the community, rather than some deviant, extreme, or isolated corner of it (unlike, for instance, dirt-bike racing, breeding llamas, or collecting old and rare violins). This brings us to our next question. Perhaps barbershop has a marginal status within the world of work itself.

One answer is yes, to the extent that serious leisure has worklike qualities but is nevertheless not work. Another answer, however, is no, for barbershoppers seldom allow their hobby to take precedence over their jobs. Barbershop is not marginal to work in this sense because barbershop singers separate their singing from their work so that the two can never compete, as barbershop sometimes does in the family. Of the eleven employed men, only four said they suffered occasional or frequent conflict between their jobs and their barbershop activities. Two of these four travelled a great deal.

Of the nine women employed full-time outside the home, five or 55.5 per cent, compared with four or 36 per cent of the working men, encountered the sort of work-leisure conflict just described. Moreover, the five were not holding down jobs requiring extensive travel. Instead they worked in subordinate positions where the hours were controlled by someone else. Still, these women said that their superiors were generally sympathetic to their leisure interests, even if they did sometimes have difficulty finding substitutes (e.g., for a private secretary or an administrative assistant) when the women wanted time off for barbershop activities. The men, presumably, would have suffered similarly had they been employed in comparable occupations, but they were not. They were more likely to be independently employed or employed in jobs such as manager or supervisor where they could manipulate their hours of work to accommodate their leisure projects.

But in general barbershop singers, in conformity with their amateur counterparts, are attracted to work that seldom, if ever, hinders the pursuit of their serious leisure.[14] And like the amateurs, work comes first in any showdown between work and barbershop. That is, barbershop singers are hardly inclined to call into work to say that they are sick and then board an early flight for a weekend convention. Thus the condition of marginality is rarely evident in the form of schedule, or role, conflict between work and serious leisure.

Marginality *is* evident, however, in the mental and physical state in which many working singers find themselves when they consider whether to attend an evening rehearsal at the end of a day on the job. Sixty per cent of the overall sample said they were sometimes or frequently fatigued from their hours at work, but still felt they should go to the rehearsal after dinner. They wanted to stay home, even though they knew from past experience that they would enjoy themselves once the music got under way – a clear conflict of values. Moreover, the rehearsals themselves can be tiring, inasmuch as good singing requires extensive use of the respiratory system and therefore a considerable expenditure of energy. Finally, barbershop choruses and quartets stand while rehearsing and performing. Lengthy periods of time on one's feet can result in backache, especially among older people and those who are overweight. A veteran singer described her ambivalence towards this situation:

> At times I'm real tired after work and have no interest in going across town to a rehearsal. But I need the practice to learn my parts. And I find that once I'm there, I'm rejuvenated. I'm happy that I went, and feel good that I am doing my part for the chorus.

A male choral singer with four years of experience in barbershop singing made similar comments:

> It's real hard after working all day. Especially, you know, if its cold outside or snowing or something like that. It's just nicer to stay home. But, you know, I really enjoy it when I go [to the rehearsal] ... I forget all about work and get into the music.

People are seldom too tired for casual leisure, nor do they usually feel obligated to undertake it. As serious leisure practitioners many barbershop singers are clearly marginal in these two ways. Incidentally, being fatigued for work the day after a rehearsal, weekend convention, or short string of evening shows – a complaint of a somewhat smaller proportion of the employed singers in the overall sample – is not another indicator of the marginality of this hobby. Casual leisure participants can overdo in this sense as well, as seen, for example, in late week-nights spent at a party, at a concert, or even before the television set.

Leisure

The marginal nature of serious leisure in general was considered in the introduction to this chapter. Here we examine those aspects of barbershop in particular that marginalize it within the social institution of leisure. In part, its marginality revolves around one very common way in which we in Western society conceive of singing – as a musical expression of joy or happiness shared with others in a convivial gathering of friends or relatives. Singing in this sense is widespread; among the examples are Christmas carolling, piano bar sing-alongs, and camp-fire songfests. It also encompasses singing in church, at parties, while marching in a military unit, and with the family after dinner. No small number of barbershop neophytes enter their hobby under the infuence of this casual leisure orientation towards song, which clashes head-on with the serious leisure orientation of many veteran members of the local chapter. Here the singer comes face to face with ambiguity through value conflict.

Likewise, and in parallel with this notion of singing as an expression of joy in the warm and friendly company of others, it was found that a barbershop chorus rehearsal is sometimes seen as the equivalent of a night out with the boys or the girls. The view of a significant number of newcomers is that it is a happy, after-work occasion where members of the same sex gather to sing and chat.[15] Although I lack direct evidence on the matter, it is likely that the neophytes who look on barbershop in this manner have little or no prior experience with serious leisure of any kind. The thought that people might undertake certain leisure activities with a sense of necessity, commitment, or even obligation, is foreign to them.

It is possible, too, that a casual orientation towards choral singing is further nurtured in the local church choirs, which serve as a major recruitment pool for North American barbershop choruses. A number of male and female respondents mentioned the 'less businesslike' approach followed in church choirs in comparison with barbershop choruses.[16] As a result, new barbershoppers who have sung in these choirs for several years often bring with them the happiness and conviviality orientation towards song as specially fashioned in this setting.

Just how marginal barbershop really is as a form of leisure can be seen in the contrast between the casual orientation of friendly singing (including the typical church choir) and the following statement of purpose. The statement is taken from the 1986 edition of the judging manual prepared by the Sweet Adelines Incorporated, the name by which the society was known before it was changed to the Sweet Adelines International:

> Sweet Adelines, Inc. is interested in establishing and maintaining the very highest musical standards possible. In order to achieve these heights, as is true in any other form of music, technical proficiency must be developed. Of equal importance, however, is the performer's ability to USE technique to project emotion through the music presented, to portray a story, to create, through the artistry of song, a truly meaningful experience.

Conclusion

The adjective 'ambiguous' describes as precisely as any word can what is marginal about the role of the barbershop singer and, to generalize tentatively, the role of all hobbyists. Very often the singer's friends, relatives, workmates, and neighbours are profoundly unclear about what he or she does and why he or she does it with such passion. In short, they are unclear about who this person really is. Work, family, and serious leisure pull barbershoppers in two, if not, three directions, making time demands that often exceed the total available discretionary hours. Moreover, the cherished values of barbershop sometimes clash with certain family and leisure values held with equal fervour by the singer's significant others.

Additionally, community-wide institutional support for the barbershop singer's leisure interests is clearly absent. This is precisely the kind of support that helps sustain serious involvement in family and work activities. For instance, such widely accepted values as being a good provider or a hard worker or being family oriented, values with which we justify our efforts in these spheres, are simply not there in the hobbyist pursuits, just as they are missing in amateurism. Furthermore, their very existence in the institutions of work and family threatens hobbyist involvements in the institution of leisure by forcing would-be participants to confront them when their avocations call them away.

Turning to the marginality hypothesis, the present study strongly suggests that committed barbershop singers and possibly other hobbyists too are marginal to the institution of leisure itself. In other words they implicitly or explicitly reject many of the values, attitudes, and patterns of behaviour associated with casual leisure, which, from the standpoint of the general population, is the core of the leisure institution. Like marginal people everywhere they consequently lack in significant degree such institutional supports for these sentiments and behaviours as respect, understanding, and encouragement.

Barbershop singers, by the way, generally seem quite undisturbed by the marginality of their leisure. They see it as a harmless social difference of which they are indeed rather proud. They are committed to a deeply fulfilling serious leisure activity in an era when most people are committed only to the comparatively superficial pursuit of pure fun. They wear this badge of distinction, you might say, with pride, even while most of the other people in their lives have some difficulty understanding the values and motives that undergird their love for the old songs.

CHAPTER SEVEN

Dissonance in Close Harmony

The three major barbershop societies have had over the years a number of successes of which they can be most proud. On the most general plane they have not only survived but also flourished, notwithstanding changes in taste in popular music, cycles of economic boom and bust, and advances in relevant technology (especially in the areas of sound recording, sound transmission, and electronic communication). More particularly, they have expanded their functions from singing purely for the joy it brings to instructing on how to sing, to educating the public about barbershop song, to giving detailed performance evaluations, to producing sophisticated choreography and stage presence and, for SPEBSQSA and Harmony, Incorporated, to supporting major charities.

All three societies have developed into international entities, which turn out a variety of periodical and occasional publications and which hold vibrant international contests and conventions fed by nearly as vibrant areal, regional, and district meetings. The men's Society operates a library and a museum, as well as a mail-order service for barbershop music, records, supplies, and gifts, all of which can be selected from a 93-page colour catalogue (1995 edition). The Sweet Adelines runs a similar, albeit somewhat less extensive and elaborate, service called the Harmony Bazaar.

Even from this partial list of successes one cannot help gaining the impression that, sociologically speaking, the art of barbershop is currently very much alive and well. The hustle and bustle observed at the conventions lends additional credibility to this impression. Moreover, many barbershop singers appear to share it. For instance, only 17 per cent of a random sample of new SPEBSQSA members interviewed for the 1993 Dieringer study saw as problematic the dissonant aspects of the social world of barbershop discussed in this chapter.[1]

Despite this admirable record of successes, however, the leaders and the rank and file of both sexes in barbershop have identified four major problems. If left unresolved they are serious enough to substantially diminish the number of enthusiasts who will take up the hobby in the future. The problems centre on membership size, membership composition, competition and excellence, and style change. The four are intricately interrelated; a change in one is likely to effect a change in one or more of the others. It is true that still other problems disturb the social world of barbershop (e.g., sexism, chapter politics, weak leadership), but most singers qualify them as less serious and as less consequential than the four considered in this chapter.[2]

Membership Size

Concern about membership abounds in all three barbershop societies. In North America, at least, membership growth has been alarmingly slower than that of the general population. According to a SPEBSQSA report written in 1988, real annual growth in its membership has consistently declined at an annual rate of 0.86 per cent since 1976. By contrast, its membership grew annually at a rate of 0.9 per cent from 1954 through 1976.[3] Between 1976 and 1993 the number of members in the Society dropped from approximately 37,000 to approximately 34,000, even though the North American male population was growing steadily throughout this period. What is worse, the Society suffers an annual drop-out rate of 25 per cent, even though the rate of retained members hovers between 86 and 88 per cent. Understandably, figures like these worry SPEBSQSA officials.

The situation has been in some respects even more grave in the Sweet Adelines International. They registered 32,000 members in 1986, but by April 1993 their numbers had shrunk to just over

28,000.[4] As for their rate of turnover it was 21 per cent in 1984, which is, however, lower than that of SPEBSQSA. Moreover, a new Sweet Adelines recruitment program, entitled 'Singing as a Way to Grow,' resulted in a 2 per cent gain in members in 1993. It was in recognition of their own problems of dwindling membership that the two female societies decided to join with SPEBSQSA in inviting sociologist Max Kaplan to organize a team of social scientists to study the matter. The team, which was formed in 1988, published the results of its research in 1993, some of which has been cited in various parts of this book.[5] One of the conclusions to be drawn from reading the different selections in the Kaplan anthology is that the size of a barbershop organization's membership is heavily influenced by the other three problems treated in this chapter.

Membership Composition

Membership composition as a problem manifests itself primarily along three dimensions, those of age, race, and sex. The first is widely recognized and widely discussed in barbershop by both the leaders and the rank and file. The opposite must be said for the race dimension; it remains hidden. It is, with certain notable exceptions, seldom mentioned in the formal reports or talked about in informal barbershopper conversations. The sex dimension was tackled by SPEBSQSA in January 1994 at a meeting of the International Board, which approved the admission of female chorus directors on a nonmember basis. At the same meeting the board also approved a new associate member category, which gives women, and certain other special categories, limited participation in the affairs of the Society. We shall start with the age dimension.

The absence of young adults in barbershop is conspicuous although, if the two Calgary samples are typical, the absence is somewhat greater among the men than among the women. The mean age of the samples reflects this demographic fact: 45.6 for the women, 49.8 for the men. These means are calculated within the age ranges of twenty-five to seventy-five and thirty-two to seventy-five for the two sexes.[6] Nineteen per cent, or three, of the women were below age thirty. The male sample contained no men in their twenties.

On the racial dimension, the absence of black and Asian singers in barbershop is glaring to those who look for equal racial representation in everyday public activities. True, for many white North Americans this absence would pass unnoticed, unless someone were to make an issue of it. That is precisely what happened in 1959 when Harmony, Incorporated seceded from the Sweet Adelines because the latter instituted a whites-only policy (see chapter 2). Now this dimension of membership composition has surfaced once again - this time among the men – in Lynn Abbott's analysis of the black history of barbershop singing:

> In the early years of its history, the national office of SPEBSQSA discouraged black membership, and thus divorced itself from possible contact with African-American roots [of barbershop]. When a Harlem-based quartet called the Grand Central Red Caps won a SPEBSQSA-sponsored singing contest in New York City in 1941, they were denied the right to compete in the national finals at St. Louis.[7]

Although Abbott could write that 'the SPEBSQSA's racial policies are vastly improved from those formative years' (p. 297), nonwhite singers are still rare in the North American chapters of the three societies. I observed thirteen quartets and twenty-one choruses at the 1993 International convention of SPEBSQSA, which together offer a good cross-sectional view of the Society. The vast majority of the quartets and many of the choruses were exclusively white. The remainder contained one or two nonwhite members at most. My observations of the quartets and choruses at the male and female regional and district conventions in which the Calgary chapters participated revealed similar ratios. The random sample of SPEBSQSA members interviewed for the 1993 Dieringer Report was 96.8 per cent white.[8]

How can we explain the observed racial imbalance in membership composition in North American barbershop? First of all, no evidence exists to support the idea that the present male and female singers are, as a group, intentionally discriminatory towards nonwhites. Indeed today, the three barbershop organizations explicitly invite all people of the appropriate sex to join them; the only exclusionary criterion is that a prospective member must have an interest in the art itself. But since official statements of this sort can be unofficially subverted, it is necessary to consider actual recruitment practices.

A look at actual practice reveals an indirect, unintentional bias in recruitment, which works in the following way. Both the Calgary study and the 1993 Dieringer Report confirm the observation that a significant majority of men and women enter the social world of barbershop through contact with a friend, workmate, or relative.[9] But it is well known that family and friendship circles in North America tend to be racially homogeneous, suggesting in turn that recruitment to the art proceeds along the same lines. The music director of the Louisville chapter, Ken Hatton, in his plea for a better racial balance in his chorus, wrote the following:

> I personally believe there is another reason [for discrimination]; our own life experiences are not racially diverse. When we invite guests to rehearsal, we choose people with whom we work, worship or socialize. Evidently, for most of us no framework exists in our lives which gives us the opportunity to develop personal relationships with men of other races. We must create our own framework.[10]

In short, the typical modern North American barbershop singer may be no more or no less racially biased than the typical member of the population in general, in the sense of preferring to be with his or her own kind.

If this hypothesis is correct then the preference works in both directions. All racial groups can be considered discriminatory in this regard, and consequently other racial groups would generally not be inclined to join an effectively all-white barbershop chapter. Moreover, it is possible that this disinclination is reinforced by the ways in which prospective nonwhite members are invited to join a local chapter. Among those ways are the impersonal calls for singers that chapters place in the local mass media and the programs of their annual shows. And, unlike the men and women who come to the chapter rehearsal hall in the company of a barbershop friend or relative, members of other racial groups must typically come alone.

Still, it appears that they might be more welcome than they think, for the Dieringer analysts found over 38 per cent of its respondents agreeing with the statement that the Society should take steps to appeal to nonwhites.[11]

In addition, apart from the blacks in North America, other nonwhite groups there generally appear to lack the same profound contact with and feeling for the traditional 'old songs' that at least some native-born whites have acquired in the course of growing up in Canada and the United States. Or, in the more extreme case, the tradition of barbershop song may quite simply be foreign to these other nonwhite groups and therefore it may quite possibly be unappealing to them. One question worth addressing in future research, then, is the extent to which, let us say, the Chinese, Mexican, or East-Asian North Americans really are interested in this form of music. Have they as ethnic groups become sufficiently socialized to North American culture to value barbershop as an art, whether as listeners or as practitioners?

Competition and Excellence

Recent surveys undertaken by or conducted for SPEBSQSA indicate that a significant minority of its members believe the Society in general and the local chapter in particular place too much emphasis on choral excellence as this quality is judged in district and international contests.[12] In 1988 the SPEBSQSA Select Committee on the Status and Future of the Society concluded:

> We are overemphasizing chorus competition, and not placing enough emphasis on learning how to perform well (viz., at annual chapter shows). Inequities exist in the C[ontest] & J[udging] system's approach to judging small and large choruses in the same setting/contest. Large choruses, which do not represent the majority of our chapters, garner a disproportionate share of the rewards in our current system, so we must find other ways of rewarding musical excellence and growth. (p. 21)

Although the surveys were not couched in these terms, they nonetheless suggest that this complaint is far more common among participants than devotees. Indeed the 1993 Dieringer survey did indicate (p. 31) that young, unmarried singers were more in favour of the pursuit of excellence and its expression in competition than their older, married colleagues.

All three barbershop societies face this problem, which is especially difficult to solve. It is not as if individual members are left to develop themselves as capable a cappella singers. We have seen that workshops, retreats, and occasional individualized instruction are available for those who want to improve in this area and thereby become better competitors. We have also seen that artistic improvement is a strong value in the social world of barbershop.[13]

But choral contests are not won solely on the strength of individual singing excellence; they are also won on the strength of such collective qualities as fine stage presence, balance of sound, and interpretation of music. To achieve this may require many more hours of rehearsal than some members have available for this purpose. One SPEBSQSA member recently wrote to *The Harmonizer*:

> If you think I'm one of the people in favor of chapter meetings being purely for musical reasons ... without any camaraderie or quartetting, you'd be very wrong ... It's just that I'm there to sing as my first order of business ... On the other hand, I don't have the inclination (and perhaps the ability) to belong to a chapter (let alone a quartet) that goes to international contests. My hat's off to you folks, but from what I've heard of how often and how hard you folks rehearse, it's just way too much for me ... Not to mention that I just don't want to work that hard at a hobby. This seems to match the views of many of the younger folks in my chapter, though some of those gents probably would mildly disagree ... The answer would seem to be that not everybody wants the same things out of the hobby.[14]

This correspondent is reacting, in part, to the problem that emerges when only a small proportion of the chorus can read music, a common situation in barbershop. As a result, learning a set of tunes for a contest usually absorbs considerable time. Consequently, it is not long before a significant number of singers, particularly the good ones, become weary of the repetition. This in turn becomes one of the principal justifications for starting an elite chorus composed of the best singers in the community who can be persuaded to join.

Satisfying this differential interest in achieving excellence and in expressing it in some sort of competition is an intractable problem found in many, if not all, of the collective amateur and hobbyist undertakings.[15] Here, where the achievements, and possibly even the social integration, of the group are dependent on the efforts of its individual members, the comparatively poor preparation, low motivation, and mediocre talent of some of them can spoil the serious fun of their more devoted and talented leisure-time collaborators. It takes a great deal of tolerance on the part of both categories if the group is to remain intact and serve as their collective vehicle of artistic or athletic expression. Even then, in large communities where sufficient athletic and artistic talent exists, splinter groups such as the elite chorus in barbershop get established sooner or later. Providing that room can be found for them, amateurs and hobbyists can now choose to join the group that is the most compatible with their level of talent and motivation.

As unsettling as the departure of a segment of a chorus can be when it occurs, the establishment of two, or even three, choruses demanding different levels of excellence and commitment to competition may be the only feasible way to solve the competence and excellence problem. The most proficient choruses would surely want to compete in their society's contests. And it follows that they would search for members whose motivation is consistent with this lofty goal. The other choruses would then be free to sing together once a week for the pure enjoyment of the music, and perhaps work towards the production of an annual show and the occasional community singout, neither of which is competitive.

Style Change

The three barbershop societies exist to promote and, for the men, to preserve barbershop song, an art that has obvious harmonic and structural roots in certain forms of nineteenth-century American popular music. Thanks to the efforts of the societies, the barbershop form now dominates the unaccompanied four-part harmony scene in North America. Still, interest in other forms has always existed and it appears that this interest is stronger today than ever. Consequently, defining the musical essence of barbershop and the theoretical limits of its evolution have become two of the most prickly issues facing the art.

People who want to sing a more dissonant music, a music with a longer melody line, or a music otherwise different from standard barbershop, or who want to depart from that style, find themselves in conflict with the goals and policies of their society. One personal solution to this impasse is to leave the local chapter to join or establish a more acceptable ensemble. This is almost always more easily said than done. For those who do carry it off, this is certainly the end of their career in barbershop as this music is traditionally defined, but it is only a turning point in the broader serious leisure career of singing in general.

An alternative is to start another society more consistent in philosophy with one's tastes in barbershop. This appears to have been the justification for establishing in the 1950s the Society of Women Barber Shop Quartet Singers in America (see chapter 2). At present the men in North America share their social world of barbershop with two small, nonaffiliated groups, which owe their existence to the minority of dissatisfied SPEBSQSA members, and a specialized subsidiary, which is officially part of the Society.

The Pioneers started in 1982 with an annual weekend retreat, which is held today in two locations, Boston and Chicago. Their goals are to promote barbershop quartet singing as a free art form, especially as it was expressed in the form of woodshedding in the days before competition became so important, and to sing the old songs that characterized the art at its inception rather than the 'trite' originals more recently composed by barbershop singers. The GUBOS group (Give Us Back Our Society) was formed in 1988 for similar reasons, to encourage quartet singing and in this manner preserve the art. GUBOS regards barbershop chorus singing as a distinctly different style.[16] The Ancient and Harmonious Society of Woodshedders (AHSOW), which was organized in 1978 around the love for improvisational barbershop, constitutes a third alternative to the art as officially practised in SPEBSQSA. Nevertheless, its members have chosen to remain within the Society as one of its subsidiaries, as did the members of AHSOW's predecessor, the Wood-shedders Guild, founded in 1958.

The Sweet Adelines and SPEBSQSA are both searching for solutions to this problem. The first has already taken a step in this direction by modifying certain procedures at its international convention. Choruses and quartets are now allowed to experiment in the 'Performance Package' segment of the competition, an innovation made possible perhaps by the broader frame of reference of the Sweet Adelines International in comparison with that of SPEBSQSA.[17] Meanwhile, the latter is aware of the problem, as is evident in a set of recommendations presented in their 'Strategic Plan' of 1988:

> We should place less emphasis on preserving our style and more on perpetuating it, by singing only songs that lead themselves to barbershop harmonization ... good, not trite, songs that audiences either recognize or can understand easily. We need to accept a broad definition of 'barbershop' (not limited by current C[ontest] &J[udging] standards) so as to 'preserve' without stifling creativity or boring our audiences.[18]

Until these recommendations are implemented, emphasis, particularly at SPEBSQSA, remains on preserving the old songs, on tradition. In their effort to preserve the traditional form, however, the societies are alienating many young adults as well as some disenchanted older adults. This is happening at a time in North American musical history when a wide gap has developed between the forms of nineteenth-century popular music in which barbershop took root and the jazzlike, electronically produced popular music of the 1980s and 1990s. The 1993 Dieringer study showed that just over 22 per cent of their sample felt that the Society should tolerate a wider variety of music.[19] Bill Seibel, a SPEBSQSA member of forty years, is in this number:

> Society for the Preservation and Encouragement of Barber Shop Singing in America? ... I think that the time has come to drop the Q

> ... First, recognize that barbershop singing, our unique brand of four-part harmony, is the unifying principle in whatever we do. This means we must quit quarreling about how individual singers choose to exercise the principle. Define our singing somewhat more broadly, if necessary, to include alternatively acceptable sub-sets, some for contest, others for performance, as Society arrangements have, in fact, been distinguished for quite some time. Our tent should be made indefinitely flexible so that members are offered the widest possible range of options. So, secondly ... the same sort of cumulative strength that occurred when singers moved into formal choruses will be found by consolidating men's and women's barbershopping ... For the old stereotypes of men and women barbershoppers mixing are no longer valid, if indeed there was ever any validity to them.[20]

Yet the fear prevails in barbershop circles that the old music will disappear if its custodians let down their guard and allow other forms of unaccompanied four-part harmony to enter the fold. How realistic is this fear?

Let us return to jazz, which was represented in chapter 1 as another original American music form. When it began to evolve in the 1920s from what is known today as its traditional, or dixieland, form, no individual or organization capable of successfully preserving that form was operating at the time. Perhaps this is why traditional jazz temporarily lost its popular appeal (which, however, it regained in the 1940s). Today it is considered one of several vibrant styles of the music.[21] The same historical pattern can be seen in classical music, one style of which even provided the harmonic and theoretical foundation for barbershop. Baroque, an early classical style, currently enjoys considerable popularity. The innovations in jazz and classical music that became the basis for new styles were rarely lauded by the musical establishment of the day, which was powerless to stop their development anyway. Yet all is well that ends well: resistance was everywhere but the new styles triumphed nonetheless. They also failed, however, to supplant their progenitors.

But jazz and classical music were never as controlled through organizations as modern barbershop. The three societies offer many services regarded by most practitioners as indispensable for the production of their art: coaching, printed music, financial support, opportunities for personal musical development, and artistic exposure (at contests and annual shows). All this is made available in the highly appealing atmosphere of camaraderie with other chapter members. Although not impossible it is nonetheless difficult to do the barbershop of today without the aid of one of the societies. They have, in short, a significant degree of control over the production of their music, and for that reason they can force members to accept their definition of what is acceptable barbershop. New styles can never take root under these conditions.

Thus it seems that the next move lies with the societies to loosen the reins somewhat. This might be accomplished by holding contests for *free* as well as for traditional barbershop.[22] The free form of quartet singing might be done in the style of the Mills Brothers or, even farther from tradition, in that of the Nylons or the black New Orleans group Seduction.[23] Free barbershop could also allow for performances by mixed-sex units. The common ground linking the different styles could perhaps be the simple requirement that all songs be interpreted within the framework of unaccompanied four-part vocal harmony. It would be up to the societies to determine the specific ways of implementing this proposal, so that those quartets and choruses who perform free barbershop would still have to do their share of preserving the traditional style. An opportunity to sing different styles might just be all that it takes to attract more youth and young adults and gain back some of the disenchanted middle-aged members. What is needed at this point in the history of barbershop is an artistic safety valve, a role that free barbershop could conceivably fill.

Conclusions

What remedies can the present study suggest for the problems of membership size and composition? Not many, it turns out. Since most barbershop singers find their way into the hobby through contacts with friends and acquaintances, recruitment efforts should try to exploit these ties. Chapter members might describe to their friends at work and to those with whom they share their leisure the excitement they find in singing. Relatives should also hear about these feelings and, in particular, the excitement should be communicated to colleagues in church choirs. For female singers, the high school glee clubs in their community may be an untapped source. A singout or two each year at different high schools by quartets and choruses of both sexes would give barbershop exposure in an area of the community where recruitment is weakest. Chapters might also perform at nearby colleges and universities and try to gain a spot on local or even regional television, a medium that confers considerable prestige.

In an attempt to solve one critical aspect of the problems of size and membership composition, both SPEBSQSA and the Sweet Adelines have recently instituted special youth programs. The former established the Harmony Explosion program, whose object is to work through the local chapters to establish a cappella clubs for high school and university men.[24] The Sweet Adelines now sponsors several youth-oriented programs through its Youth Singers Foundation. These include the Bev Sellers Memorial Scholarship for vocal music students and the Young Women in Harmony Program, which is dedicated to the enrichment of music education in the schools.

One of the oft-heard arguments in barbershop circles goes like this: young adults are generally not attracted to barbershop because it is so dramatically different from the popular music that they and their peers are so fond of. Nevertheless, some older teenagers and young adults do take a substantial interest in other less-than-popular forms of music, notably jazz and classical music. A certain number of these listeners even become vocal or instrumental performers of such music on an amateur or professional basis. Casual observation suggests further that 'unusual' musical interests of this sort are often sustained in parallel with the dominant peer group tastes in popular music. These segments of the late teenage and young adult population appear to be leading a quite comfortable dual musical existence. Is there any reason why some of the people in this age category could not accommodate themselves in a similar manner to the currently uncommon combination of barbershop and popular music? The youth programs are in reality based on the assumption that such an accommodation is possible.

CHAPTER EIGHT

Musical Lifestyles

A common thread links the social world of barbershop with the neighbouring social worlds of jazz and classical music as these were sketched in the first chapter. The common thread is the general musical lifestyle shared by the musicians who inhabit one or more of these three. Indeed a far greater diversity of musicians than those considered in this book can be found in this lifestyle, which may be defined as the musicians' special way of living that gives each one of them a sense of communion with the others, however different the music they play. The musicians who share this lifestyle have in common their pursuit of a fine or popular art, rather than the pursuit of a type of folk music (of the noncommercial variety). Those who pursue the latter hold to a substantially different way of life, which I will not examine here as that would take us too far afield.[1] But by comparing the lifestyles of jazz and classical musicians with the lifestyle of barbershop singers, we can discover important similarities and differences between them and in this way broaden our sociological understanding of the latter.

After reviewing the lifestyle literature, much of which is found in the field of leisure studies, I developed the following definition:

> A lifestyle is a distinctive set of shared patterns of tangible behavior that is organized around a set of coherent interests or social conditions or both, that is explained and justified by a set of related values, attitudes, and orientations and that, under certain conditions, be-

comes the basis for a separate, common social identity for its participants.[2]

Among sociologists, the tendency has existed for some time to study these acticities at the individual level and, at times, to generalize from there to activities practised by entire collectivities. This study of barbershop singers was guided primarily by the search for shared patterns of behaviour, although I learned in the course of it that the interviewees commonly link certain values, attitudes, and orientations to the activities constituting their lifestyles. In everyday life it is difficult to separate the actions of people from the motives and personal meanings they use to explain and justify those actions.[3]

Glyptis's review of the social science literature on lifestyles turned up only a handful of empirical explorations of the idea.[4] This research tends to be mainly descriptive, centring as it does on the everyday social habits of different groups and categories of people. Additionally, Veal notes that lifestyles are fundamentally cultural in scope.[5] In other words, in this area of study the investigator focuses chiefly on the patterns of routine activities as they are enacted within the framework of formal and informal social organization and, as the preceding definition indicates, the values, attitudes, and orientations people use to explain and justify these activities.

We examined David Unruh's conception of the social world in chapter 1, where it was applied to the fields of jazz, barbershop, and classical music. It appears that Unruh overlooked not only the cultural side of the concept of social world but also its constituent lifestyles, which could be argued to be one of its most important components. True, he did touch on the idea when he observed that they 'must be seen as an internally recognizable constellation of actors, organizations, events, and *practices*' (emphasis mine). But this is as far as he went.

Were it not for the unfortunate omission of culture, he might have seen that the idea of lifestyle dovetails nicely with that of social world as it has been presented and elaborated throughout this book. That is, the two concepts go together so long as we are concentrating not on the lifestyles of individual musicians but on the lifestyles of categories of musicians – on the ways of living observed among the musicians in jazz, barbershop, classical music, and their combinations.

The Shared Lifestyle

One patch of common ground shared by those who perform jazz, barbershop, and classical music is the requirement of routine individual practice. The best musicians in these fields practise daily or very nearly so, always in face of the possibility that too long a lapse here could lead to a dispiriting atrophy of ability. All three social worlds are further united by the persistent need to learn new music and to develop and maintain satisfactory technique. They are also united by the widely held attitude that practising is considerably less enjoyable than performing before an audience.

On the collective level the practice session finds its equivalent in the rehearsal, where, in the typical case, an ensemble tries to perfect a selection of works for public consumption. Rehearsals are common in all three forms of music. So are the various occasions of spontaneously organized music such as the jam session in jazz, the on-the-spot singing of tags and even entire songs in barbershop, and the forming of temporary chamber ensembles for an evening's enjoyment in classical music. And whereas many of these musicians seem to enjoy their rehearsals more than their sessions of personal practice, they commonly single out their concerts as the most exhilarating part of their musical existence, with the spontaneous sessions defined as the next most exhilarating. In the concerts they present the works they have striven so hard to polish and at the same time search for the enthusiastic audience approval that can so greatly enhance their sense of enrichment.

The polar opposites of stage fright and eager anticipation are universal concomitants of the public performance. Stage fright is genuine fear; it occurs when performers worry that a slip in their presentation will be spotted by the general audience or a critical observer.[6] My research reveals that it most commonly afflicts inexperienced musicians who are in the process of learning how to control it.[7] These musicians eventually learn what veterans in the three arts learned many years earlier – public performance, because it is so exhilarating, is something to be eagerly anticipated. Instead of being repelled or gripped by fear, the veterans are attracted by a small number of powerful, uncommon rewards such as the successful emotional communication of musical meanings and the public approval that this communication can bring. Sufficient practising and rehearsing can contribute greatly to the reduction of stage fright and the parallel emergence of eager anticipation.

Yet another characteristic of the shared musical lifestyle of these three arts is their nonseasonal nature. This observation also appears to hold for nearly all of the fine and popular arts, whereas it clearly fails to hold for a number of other amateur and hobbyist endeavours, such as found in sport and science. Still, there are orchestral seasons, and some barbershop choruses do not normally rehearse or perform in the summer.[8]

Musicians in all three arts are inclined to pursue their music throughout the year. Many classical musicians continue to practise during the summer, while seeking chamber groups as outlets for their talents. Committed barbershop singers do much the same, except that they search for singing opportunities in quartets and church choirs. Jazz musicians quite obviously lack even this minor change of pace. Rather they may be busiest in December and early January, when most amateur orchestras and some barbershop choruses rehearse and perform rather little. But it is also true that during this time of the year they probably play more commercial dance music than jazz.

Finally, musicians in jazz, barbershop, and classical music are indefatigable consumers of their own art. Beginners have to listen extensively just to learn it; established musicians want to listen extensively because they appreciate it. For both categories, part of the accompanying leisure or professional lifestyle consists of sitting before a stereo, radio, or television set, where they take in mediated presentations of their music. This background is augmented by attending live performances held locally or wherever they can be conveniently found.

Distinctive Lifestyles

Beyond this common core of practices, lifestyles in jazz, barbershop, and classical music diverge sharply. For example, consider the different roles that family members play in the three arts. In classical music they may play together at home in various ensembles, whereas the equivalent involvement in barbershop is much less common, whether at home or in the local chapter. In the latter by comparison, substantial family participation is available through the many volunteer roles associated with this form of music. For instance, a member of a barbershopper's family might take tickets or work backstage at the annual show, assist at an after-glow, or help the singer perfect his or her part. Although an interest in performing jazz may be passed from one generation to the next (e.g., the Marsalis family of New Orleans), most musicians in this art do not perform at jam sessions or concerts with members of their family. Rather the main family role here is one of listener, which is filled in large measure by spouses or partners. They also make up the major proportion of the audiences at barbershop and amateur classical music performances.

The social milieu within which each art is produced is equally divergent. This milieu consists of a distinctive set of practices that constitute an important part of the overall lifestyle of the art. Let us turn first to jazz, which is still most commonly performed as either a one-night stand or a multiple-night engagement in a night-club or restaurant.

Here the music is presented in 'sets,' the length of which is determined to some extent by the convention that musicians take a ten-minute break for every hour they perform. Whereas individual jazz groups may decide to break less frequently, periodic breaks at some point are needed to rest lips and fingers. During these pauses the musicians soon fall into comfortable routines, drinking beer or coffee, talking with patrons, discussing their profession, having a smoke, or, if the club is so equipped, listening to jazz on the jukebox. The small jazz ensembles, or 'combos' as they are sometimes referred to, may rehearse from time to time, but they rarely do so with the regularity known in barbershop, classical music, and big-band jazz.

Among the other practices differentiating jazz musicians from barbershop singers and classical musicians are two that are especially familiar to those who know the social world of the jazz musicians – accepting requests from the audience and inviting visiting musicians to 'sit in,' or play briefly with the band. The jam session, whether held during the day or early in the morning after a club gig, is still most commonly found where it originated, in the world of jazz.

Jazz musicians also present concerts, as do the other singers and instrumentalists considered here, but sometimes they do so as part of a festival. Festivals seem to be somewhat rarer in classical music and unheard of in barbershop. Festival work includes evening concerts given in large halls as well as more rough-and-ready daytime performances presented in tents or on outdoor soundstages. In addition, the better-known musicians at these festivals may direct workshops or seminars on specialized aspects of their music. Finally, jazz musicians may become involved in their local jazz club not only as occasional performers for its members but also as officers or volunteers in various service roles.

Barbershop, on the other hand, is pursued in a substantially different social milieu. Choral work normally requires the singer to attend weekly evening rehearsals, which are often held in the assembly room of a local church. The conventional break in the middle of the two to three hours set aside for this purpose is filled with talk about barbershop singing and personal matters shared with other singers. Refreshments are usually available at this time. Since the rehearsals are conducted in a space used for other activities occurring on other days, a crew must be established to assemble and disassemble the risers on which the singers stand during much of the evening.

Quartets normally rehearse once a week in someone's home, where they follow the same convention of breaking at midpoint for rest and refreshments. The refreshments served on these occasions are similar to those served in amateur chamber music sessions, and are rarely, if ever, alcoholic. This is serious leisure, the conduct of which is noticeably impaired by even a slightly numbed capacity to perform.

The singouts in barbershop are roughly equivalent to the one-night stands in jazz, except that the singouts are normally much shorter, require no breaks, and are presented at irregular intervals in a wider variety of locations (e.g., schools, hospitals, shopping centres, nursing homes). The annual chapter show in barbershop – an undertaking of considerable proportions – has no equivalent in the other two arts. As distinctive are the annual regional, district, and areal conventions and allied contests. Both the shows and the contests endow weekly rehearsals with a special purpose; the rehearsals are almost exclusively geared towards perfecting the routines and songs to be performed there.

Moving beyond the core activity of making music, a sizeable percentage of barbershop singers round out their hobbyist lifestyle with an impressive range of service work. As we saw earlier some of them attend regular committee meetings or perform special functions in connection with the annual show. One of their number will be recruited to write a newsletter. A few will run in the annual election for the positions of president, treasurer, and secretary. With the exception of those musicians who become involved in the local club, such volunteer activities are unheard of in jazz. And it is little different for the small number of jazz musicians who find their way into the town's amateur community orchestra, for it is clear that the proliferation of committees and functions is noticeably less in jazz than in barbershop.

The community orchestras staffed by amateur classical musicians operate on a schedule of weekly evening rehearsals similar to barbershop, leading typically to four concerts each year rather than one grand annual show. Some of these orchestras present supplementary concerts as well, which are equivalent to singouts in barbershop and are held in such places as schools, churches, and shopping centres. The more established ensembles may even take their main programs on the road to communities usually within a day's drive of the city in which they are based.

Many amateur classical musicians organize their chamber music pursuits around their orchestral commitments. Others, being unaffiliated with an orchestra, often develop a distinctly different schedule of musical involvement. Chamber groups that perform regularly in public must likewise rehearse regularly, even though their performances, like barbershop singouts, usually take place irregularly. Nevertheless most chamber music players gather together for no other reason than to play for the pure enjoyment of it all, which may or may not happen on a regular basis. Whether or not they rehearse regularly, the small groups (they are typically composed of two to six members) are most likely to meet in someone's home, where, as observed earlier, they adhere to a pattern of breaks and refreshments similar to that of the barbershop quartets.

The Importance of Lifestyle

The social worlds of jazz, barbershop, and classical music are united by a shared lifestyle and differentiated by distinctive lifestyles. We find in the three arts a sense of kinship along with a sense of being special. The sense of being special rests not only on the fundamental differences in the forms of music themselves but also on the everyday ways in which they are produced. Put otherwise, I am arguing – at the risk of infuriating some musicologists I suspect – that the meaning of these forms of music for the performers comes as much from the lifestyles of the musicians as it does from the essential qualities of the arts they are expressing. Furthermore, the musicians find both their art and its lifestyle enormously appealing, whether considered separately or in combination.

To be precise, we can say that the two are inextricably tied to each other. As jazzman Charlie Parker so aptly observed:

> Music is your own experience, your thoughts, your wisdom. If you don't live it, it won't come out of your horn. They teach you there's a boundary line to music. But, man, there's no boundary line to art.[9]

In this sense, then, the social world that develops around a form of music is no mere auxiliary or peripheral formation, clinging like a parasite as it were to the pure art itself. Rather the art is shaped and expressed through the medium of that social world in general and through its everyday lifestyles in particular. To change metaphors, the art of music is like a two-sided coin, minted in a blend of music as experience and experience as music. Here is a fundamental truth that no musician would ever deny.

Lifestyle, Social World, and Barbershop

The study reported in this book makes it abundantly clear that the social basis of barbershop has always been, is now, and will likely continue to be exceptionally rich when compared with many other forms of Western music. The production of the music itself is inherently social. Put in the simplest terms, it cannot be made alone, and a knowledgeable, appreciative audience adds tremendously to the pleasure of making it. More to the point, the emotional experience of singing attractive, well-rehearsed melodies in close harmony with friends before an audience who enjoys the art is unique and highly memorable. This is the *barbershop experience*, the supreme value on which the social world of barbershop rests and around which the lifestyle of its members revolves. Everything else is secondary by comparison.

For those who come to know the barbershop experience first-hand, it seems highly unlikely that they will voluntarily give it up. The longevity of the social world of barbershop would thus appear to be guaranteed, so long as thousands of men and women around the world discover this experience. For, as the Calgary study suggests, once singers have had the barbershop experience, they will want to repeat it, thereby establishing it as their lifelong hobby and their special form of serious leisure. A small proportion of the members of the three societies will come and go, oblivious to the rewarding experiences that could be theirs in the social world of barbershop in which they are mere passersby. Somehow they miss what is so evident to those who have discovered it through their participation in the hobby and who have decided to stay on for more. Such turnover is to be expected, particularly in serious leisure where people will want to try out an activity for its personal fit before committing themselves to a heavy involvement in it.

Male and female barbershop will have to find a way of communicating to young people and minority groups of all ages this essential barbershop experience. Some suggestions were made in the preceding chapter. Given the staggering number of competing leisure interests that abound today, recruiting from these groups will be difficult. But the effort must be made, for declining membership can hardly be allowed to continue indefinitely. While this is going on, barbershop singers must not lose heart. They must not forget that they sing a distinctive, interesting, challenging music with which many men and women the world over can easily identify, providing they have the opportunity to hear it and try their hand at producing it.

APPENDIX

Interview Guide for the Study of Barbershop Singers

The questions in this guide were developed to further explore several important aspects of the social world of barbershop that came to my attention while observing its participants in action. These aspects include the singing career of the respondent and his or her hobbyist lifestyle. I also asked about the relationships between barbershop and family and work. Near the end of the interview we took up the subject of the costs and rewards associated with this form of serious leisure. This is the final version of the interview guide which, as is common in exploratory research, was changed along the way in response to the emergence of new leads about the nature of the lifestyle and social world of barbershop singing.

I Career

A) Can you recall when you first became interested in barbershop music as a lover or fan of it? [describe how this happened]

B) How did this initial interest continue? [get history of singing involvement to first membership in chorus or quartet]

1) Were any of your friends or relatives instrumental in your initial involvement in barbershop singing?

2) Did you have any singing experience before you entered the world of barbershop?

C) What has your involvement been since you joined your first chorus or quartet? [get history of involvement]

D) What thrills have you had in barbershop singing?

1) In this regard do you prefer choral or quartet singing?

E) What disappointments have you had in barbershop singing?

F) What are your plans for the future so far as barbershop is concerned?

II Lifestyle

A) How many hours would you estimate that you spend in a typical week in barbershop singing, including service work for the art?

B) Are you a member of the chorus (Y/N); of a quartet (Y/N); neither?

C) On the average in the past six months how many singouts have you participated in each month? [obtain for both chorus and quartet members]

D) What percentage of your close and moderately close friends and relatives are barbershop singers?

1) Are your friends and relatives in barbershop mostly in the same section (bass, tenor, etc.) in the chorus?

2) Are your friends and relatives in barbershop mostly the same age as you?

III Family and Spouse or Other Companion

A) Does your companion (spouse, friend, etc.) accept, tolerate, or reject your involvement in barbershop?

1) If he or she tolerates or rejects, what is there about the barbershop lifestyle that he or she dislikes?

B) Does your companion become involved in barbershop in any way?

C) Does the rest of your family become involved in barbershop in any way?

IV Work

A) What is your present job?

B) What is your present level of education?

C) Does your work conflict with barbershop?
If so, how?

D) Does work leave you fatigued for barbershop?

E) Does barbershop leave you fatigued for work?

F) Is barbershop often on your mind at work?

V Orientations

A) What are the rewards of barbershop singing? [present card with list of rewards to respondent]
B) What are your major dislikes in barbershop singing [indicate that I am not interested in minor peeves]
C) Do you get stagefright before performances?
If so, how do you deal with it?

VI Miscellaneous

A) What are your other hobbies, avocations?
B) How old are you?
C) [note further observations and comments from respondent]

Notes

CHAPTER 1. The Social Worlds of Music

1 Unruh, 'Characteristics and Types of Participation in Social Worlds,' 115.
2 Unruh, 'The Nature of Social Worlds,' 271–96.
3 Truzzi, 'Toward a General Sociology of the Folk, Popular, and Elite Arts,' 279–89.
4 Becker, *Art Worlds.*
5 Ibid., 307–10.
6 Randel, *The New Harvard Dictionary of Music,* 812.
7 Stebbins, *Amateurs, Professionals, and Serious Leisure,* 3. General statements throughout the study about amateurs, professionals, hobbyists, career volunteers, and serious leisure, unless noted otherwise, have been pulled from this book. It synthesizes fifteen years of research on eight different amateur-professional fields in art, science, sport, and entertainment.
8 Stebbins, 'The Liberal Arts Hobbies,' 173–86.
9 Csikszentmihalyi, *Beyond Boredom and Anxiety.*
10 Stebbins, 'Classical Music Amateurs,' 78–103.
11 Hall, 'Theoretical Trends in the Sociology of Occupations,' 5–23; Klegon, 'The Sociology of Professions,' 259–83.
12 Machlis, *The Enjoyment of Music,* 49–50; Randel, *New Harvard Dictionary of Music,* 811–12.
13 Becker, *Art Worlds,* chapter 2.
14 Buerkle and Barker, *Bourbon Street Black,* 132.
15 Souchon and Rose, *New Orleans Jazz,* 200.
16 Collier and Robinson, 'Jazz,' 535–62.
17 Stebbins, 'A Theory of the Jazz Community,' 318–31.
18 Machlis, *The Enjoyment of Music,* 50.
19 Stebbins, 'Music among Friends,' 52–73 and 'Creating High Culture,' 616–31.

20 SPEBSQSA, 'Barbershop Arranging Manual,' 3.
21 Sparkes and Wright, 'Barbershop Harmony,' 18/14. See also Abbott, '"Play That Barber Shop Chord",' 289–325.
22 'Close harmony' refers to the arrangement of vocal parts so that the notes of each chord fall within an octave.
23 Hicks, 'Barbershop Quartet Singing,' 147.
24 Martin, 'The Evolution of Barbershop Harmony,' 41.
25 SPEBSQSA, 'Barbershop Arranging Manual,' 33.
26 Barbershop is substantial in its execution but not in its form, which is appreciated precisely for its simplicity. But to sing barbershop well requires a great deal of ability, practice, and experience.

CHAPTER 2. The Old Songs

1 Abbott, '"Play That Barber Shop Chord," 289–325.
2 See, for example, Martin, 'The Evolution of Barbershop Harmony,' 40–1, 106; and Hicks, *Heritage of Harmony*, 2.
3 Dawney, 'Tonsorial Musicians,' 208–9.
4 Hicks, *Heritage of Harmony*, 4. Brandt devotes nearly a page to the subject in his chapter on woodshedding in 'The Respectable Art of Woodshedding in World Music,' 45–6. Furthermore he cites a statement on the matter written by barbershop historian Martin in *Book of Musical Americana*, 42. Finally, the Heritage Hall Museum of Barbershop Harmony at SPEBSQSA headquarters in Kenosha houses correspondence written in 1946 by Deac Martin and Joe Stern (another barbershop historian) which indicates that both men clearly understood the major role played by blacks in the origin of the art.
5 See also Hicks, 'Barbershop Quartet Singing,' 146.
6 For a discussion of the sociological meaning of profession, see Stebbins, *Amateurs, Professionals, and Serious Leisure*, chapter 2.
7 Gates, 'Barbershoppers and Music Educators,' 103–4.
8 This appears to have been the inspiration of Cash, a man renowned for his sense of humour. Snyder ('Historical Notes,' *The Harmonizer* 40, 20) provides two examples:

> The necessary evil of convention registration will take place on the mezzanine floor, Hotel Tulsa. Barbershoppers will be vaccinated, ear-tagged, and tattooed so that they can be returned to the herd if lost, strayed, or stolen.
>
> Final convention jamboree ... gang singing, novelty quartet performances, baying at the moon, etc. ... ends when the last tenor, lead, bass, or baritone drops from sheer exhaustion.

Nonetheless, SPEBSQSA leaders now believe the name and its celebrated acronym have outlived their usefulness. They have proposed that the organization be known henceforth as 'The Barbershop Harmony Society (SPEBSQSA).' See Select Committee on the Status and Future of the Society, 'A Strategic Plan for the Barbershop Harmony Society (SPEBSQSA),' 2.

9 Snyder, 'From the Inside,' 13–32.

10 Cash's club was not the first of its kind. Snyder ('Historical Notes,' *The Harmonizer* 42, 14) reports that the Illinois Harmony Club, which consisted of six chapters, was organized in 1934.

11 The official shortened name for SPEBSQSA is now the 'Barbershop Harmony Society.' Members are officially discouraged from trying to pronounce the Society's initials as though they made up an acronym.

12 Abbott, '"Play That Barber Shop Chord",' 296–7.

13 Snyder, 'Historical Notes,' *The Harmonizer* 40, 20.

14 Snyder, 'From the Inside,' 15–19.

15 Ibid., 22.

16 Ibid., 31.

17 The information in this section is taken from a Sweet Adelines publicity brochure and from a thirty-year history of the organization written by Parsons, *30 Years of Harmony*.

18 Gates, 'A Historical Comparison of Public Singing by American Men and Women,' 32–46.

19 Parsons, *30 Years of Harmony*, 34.

20 Ibid., 81.

21 In 1991 the Sweet Adelines, Incorporated changed its name to Harmony International. The threat of legal action from Harmony, Incorporated forced the latter to retreat in 1993 to its present name, Sweet Adelines International. At least two reasons lie behind the desire to change the organization's name: first, some members felt that the locution 'sweet adelines' was belittling; second, many members were eager to expand internationally, to profit from the current global interest in barbershop song being shown by both sexes.

22 The information in this section was drawn almost entirely from a twenty-five year history of the society, Harmony, Inc., 'Harmony from Our Hearts.'

CHAPTER 3. Organized Barbershop

1 See, for example, Bishop and Hoggett, *Organizing around Enthusiasms*, Olmsted, 'Hobbies and Serious Leisure,' 27–32.

2 Dieringer Research Associates, 'A Report on Telephone Interviews,' 27.

3 SPEBSQSA, 'The President,' 10.

4 This definition is developed from Van Til, *Mapping the Third Sector*, 5–9 and Fischer and Schaffer, *Older Volunteers*, 13–14.

5 See Stebbins, *Amateurs, Professionals, and Serious Leisure,* 16.
6 The SPEBSQSA also organizes a midwinter convention, which is primarily administrative. Nonetheless a senior quartet contest is held at this time along with several mini-courses on a diversity of interests dear to barbershop singers and administrators. Those in attendance are also treated to a concert by the reigning medallist quartets.
7 These statements are taken from Parsons, *30 Years of Harmony,* 3; Harmony, Incorporated, 'Harmony from Our Hearts,' inside front cover; and SPEBSQSA, 'The President,' 45.

CHAPTER 4. Becoming a Barbershop Singer

1 The decision to use exploratory methodology to study barbershop and to develop a grounded theory about the art is easily justified. To this point there has been literally no sociological research on it. Exploration in sociology is discussed by Glaser and Strauss, *The Discovery of Grounded Theory,* and Strauss, *Qualitative Analysis for Social Scientists* among others.
2 For further details on this definition see Stebbins, *Amateurs, Professionals, and Serious Leisure,* chapter 3.
3 Someone who volunteers to do a task that is largely unskilled (e.g., take tickets at a high school play, serve coffee at a reception) or give something (e.g., money, blood) is not a *career* volunteer in the sense used here.
4 See, for example, Pavalko, *Sociology of Occupations and Professions,* chapter 2.
5 This finding may not be replicated in surveys on the matter. Barbershop singers themselves, based on personal experience, believe that relatives are more important in this regard than the present study suggests. Of interest here is the somewhat broader finding from the 1993 Dieringer study that 64.4 per cent of the new members sampled first heard about the Society through a friend *or* relative. Dieringer Research Associates, 'A Report on Telephone Interviews with New Members,' 21. Kaplan discovered several two-, three-, and four-generation families of male barbershop singers in his more loosely designed study, 'SPEBSQSA's Future: Tradition and Innovation,' 130–2.
6 Neulinger, *To Leisure: An Introduction,* 188–91.
7 Dieringer Research Associates, 'Society for the Preservation and Encouragement of Barber Shop Quartet Singing in America,' 16.
8 Brandt, 'The Respectable Art of Woodshedding,' 37.
9 Dieringer Research Associates, 'A Report on Telephone Interviews with New Members,' 27.
10 Mel Knight, personal communication (29 May 1981). To my knowledge, no one has ever tried to explain why the two sexes vary on this account.
11 Precise, unison pronunciation is crucial in the production of the rounded,

ringing, consonant harmonies of traditional barbershop song. This effect is diminished, possibly even lost, when, for instance, some singers pronounce 'a' as 'ah' and others pronounce it as 'aw.' To achieve this sonority, each singer must also start and finish at precisely the same time the pronunciation and inflection of each syllable in each word.

12 Stebbins, 'Career: The Subjective Approach,' 32–49.

13 Dieringer Research Associates, 'Society for the Preservation and Encouragement of Barber Shop Quartet Singing in America,' 10.

14. Although a transferred singer can also transfer his or her membership to the new local chapter, heavy responsibilities in the new job and the probable absence of friends in the new chapter often seem to become barriers too formidable to surmount.

15 Letter to the editor, *The Harmonizer* (September/October, 1994), 38.

CHAPTER 5. Why Sing?

1 This introductory section draws from Stebbins, *Amateurs, Professionals, and Serious Leisure*, chapters 1 and 6.

2 Homans, *Social Behavior*, 31.

3 We might question whether exploration is justified in this area of sociology and psychology, where considerable attention has been given to the issue of leisure motives and benefits. Clearly it is, for the theory and data on leisure motives and benefits are much too general to inform us about the nature of these two orientations when expressed in everyday life during the pursuit of a particular form of leisure. See Stebbins, 'Costs and Rewards in Barbershop Singing,' 123–33.

4 Podilchak, 'Distinctions of Fun, Enjoyment and Leisure,' 133–48.

5 Stebbins, *Amateurs, Professionals, and Serious Leisure*, 98.

6 Csikszentmihalyi, *Beyond Boredom and Anxiety.*

7 Stebbins, *Amateurs, Professionals, and Serious Leisure*, 100–7.

8 Ibid., 9–10, 42–3.

9 See, for example, Stebbins, *The Laugh-Makers*, 85–7.

10 Lyman and Scott, *A Sociology of the Absurd*; Stebbins, 'Toward a Social Psychology of Stage Fright,' 156–63.

11 Stebbins, *Amateurs: On the Margin between Work and Leisure*, 117–18.

CHAPTER 6. Work in Leisure

1 Stebbins, *Amateurs: On the Margin between Work and Leisure* and *Amateurs, Professionals, and Serious Leisure.*

2 On commitment see also Buchanan, 'Commitment and Leisure Behavior,'

401–20, and Shamir, 'Commitment and Leisure,' 238–58. On the investment of time and energy in leisure, see Kelly, *Leisure Identities and Interactions*, 195–6.

3 As good a descriptor as this is Goffman's decision to classify the quietly disaffiliated as deviant fails to square with the amateurs' views of themselves and, for that matter, with deviance theory. See, for example, Stebbins, *Tolerable Differences: Living with Deviance* 2–7, and Goffman, *Stigma: Notes on the Management of Spoiled Identity*, 143–5.

4 Chiropractors were once described in these terms. See Wardwell, 'A Marginal Professional Role: The Chiropractor,' 339–48. For a recent discussion of marginal professions, see Ritzer and Walczak, *Working: Conflict and Change*, chapter 9.

5 Stebbins, *Amateurs, Professionals, and Serious Leisure*, chapter 7.

6 On leisure as a social institution see Dumazedier, 'Leisure and Postindustrial Societies,' 201–2; Kaplan, *Leisure: Theory and Policy*, 28–31 and Kelly, 'Sociological Perspectives and Leisure Research,' 127–58.

7 Rosenthal's study of chiropractors exemplifies this possibility in 'Marginal or Mainstream: Two Studies of Contemporary Chiropractic,' 271–85.

8 Stebbins, *Amateurs, Professionals, and Serious Leisure*, 8.

9 The mean of 1.1 excludes one exceptionally devoted male respondent who practised an average of seven hours per week. Were his hours incorporated into the calculations, the male average would raise to 1.8 hours per week.

10 Of the six married female respondents who said that their husbands accepted barbershopping, one reported 'weak' acceptance. In other words, her husband grows noticeably less accepting of it as shows and contests approach and time commitments expand accordingly.

11 The educational profile of the male singers in the Calgary study varies at times from that in the 1994 Dieringer study. In brief, when compared with the Dieringer study, somewhat more Calgarians had completed high school and a technical program, whereas fewer had completed a graduate program. About the same number were university graduates. Dieringer Research Associates, 'Society for the Preservation and Encouragement of Barber Shop Quartet Singing in America, Inc.,' 9.

12 Select Committee on the Status and Future of the Society, 'A Strategic Plan for the Barbershop Harmony Society,' 13–14.

13 Homans, *Social Behavior: Its Elementary Forms*, 307–8.

14 Stebbins, *Amateurs, Professionals, and Serious Leisure*, 112.

15 Talking and wisecracking on the risers during rehearsals were two outstanding annoyances mentioned by the directors and the committed singers. They categorically want attention focused exclusively on the former while working on a given song.

16 To be fair, one can always find barbershop choruses whose approach is more casual than serious and church choirs whose approach is more serious than casual. It is rather a matter of parallel gradation of seriousness between the two types, with more barbershop choruses falling near the seriousness end of the continuum and more church choirs falling near the opposite end. Neither type of chorus is normally found at the top of the local hierarchies of seriousness and prestige, however, for that honour commonly goes to the community's opera, symphony, and university choruses.

CHAPTER 7. Dissonance in Close Harmony

1 Dieringer Research Associates, 'A Report on Telephone Interviews with New Members,' 45.
2 Sexism was not mentioned in the 1993 Dieringer survey (p. 45) as a response to the question, 'What do you like least about the Society,' but it is talked about from time to time in barbershop circles. It also came up twice for discussion in a recent issue of *The Harmonizer*, once in a column and once in a section containing 'Letters to the Editor.' See Foster, 'Let's End "Put-Down" of Women in Our Performances,' 31, and Baker, '"Please Stop This Trend,"' 28.
3 Select Committee on the Status and Future of the Society, 'A Strategic Plan for the Barbershop Harmony Society (SPEBSQSA),' 13–14.
4 Ibid., 14.; *The Pitch Pipe* 46 (January 1994), inside front cover.
5 Kaplan (ed.), *Barbershopping: Musical and Social Harmony*.
6 At fifty-five years, the mean age in SPEBSQSA is even higher. See Select Committee on the Status and Future of the Society, 'A Strategic Plan,' 2.
7 Abbott, '"Play That Barber Shop Chord"', 296.
8 Dieringer Research Associates, 'A Report of Telephone Interviews with New Members,' 5.
9 Dieringer Research Associates, 'A Report on Telephone Interviews with the General Population,' 34–5.
10 Hatton, 'A Little More Tonal Color, Please,' 36.
11 Ibid., 47.
12 See Select Committee on the Status and Future of the Society, 'A Strategic Plan,' 21. The 1993 Dieringer survey found that 9.2 per cent of the sampled SPEBSQSA members disliked this aspect of the Society, which was by far the most prominent dislike listed there. See Dieringer Research Associates, 'A Report on Telephone Interviews with New Members,' p. 45.
13 Fifty-five per cent of the 1993 Dieringer sample indicated that this value is very important to them (p. 31).
14 Letter to the Editor, *The Harmonizer* 55 (January/February, 1995): 30.

15 Stebbins, *Amateurs, Professionals, and Serious Leisure*, 102–3.

16 The Pioneers and GUBOS are briefly discussed in the report of the Select Committee on the Status and Future of the Society, 'A Strategic Plan,' 12–13. See also Brandt, 'The Respectable Art of Woodshedding in World Music.' The interest in woodshedding can be profound for, as Brandt notes, some barbershop singers 'believe that woodshedding is not only a joyful experience, but also an important creative art form' (p. 33).

17 Sweet Adelines International has not adopted the goal of preserving barbershop. Rather it is 'a woman's organization dedicated to education and achievement through competition and performance of four-part harmony barbershop style.' See *The Pitchpipe* (1990): 16.

18 Select Committee on the Status and Future of the Society, 'A Strategic Plan,' 22.

19 Dieringer Research Associates, 'A Report on Telephone Interviews with New Members,' 47.

20 Bill Seibel, 'SPEBSSA?' *The Harmonizer* ('The Way I See It' column) 55 (March/April 1994): 30.

21 The seemingly endless lines of people trying to enter Preservation Hall in New Orleans attest to the popularity of traditional jazz. Moreover, concerts by the Preservation Hall Band are in demand across North America. See Robert A. Stebbins, *The Connoisseur's New Orleans* (Calgary, Alta.: University of Calgary Press, 1995).

22 Named after a similar arrangement in figure skating where tension between innovation and tradition is also prominent.

23 Seduction appeared briefly on CBS's 'Super Bowl Saturday Night,' 25 January 1990.

24 The precursor of Harmony Explosion was Young Men in Harmony, which was founded in 1970.

CHAPTER 8. Musical Lifestyles

1 See Lewis, 'The Sociology of Popular Culture,' 1–160, and Truzzi, 'Toward a General Sociology of the Folk, Popular, and Elite Arts,' 283–4.

2 Stebbins, 'Lifestyle as a Generic Concept in Ethnographic Research.' This definition draws substantially on the ideas of Sobel, *Lifestyle and Social Structure: Concepts, Definitions, Analyses*, 28, and Veal, 'The Concept of Lifestyle: A Review,' 233–52.

3 Zurcher, Kirkpatrick, Cushing, and Bowman, 'The Anti-Pornography Campaign: A Symbolic Crusade,' 217–38; Glyptis, *Leisure and Unemployment*, 37–8.

4 Glyptis, 'Lifestyles and Leisure Patterns – Methodological Approaches,' 106.

5 Veal, 'Leisure, Lifestyle and Status: A Pluralist Framework for Analysis,' 141–53.

6 Lyman and Scott, *A Sociology of the Absurd*; Stebbins, 'Toward a Social Psychology of Stage Fright.'

7 Stebbins, *Amateurs, Professionals, and Serious Leisure*, chapter 6.

8 The amount of activity in barbershop choruses and quartets during the summer and around the Christmas–New Year's period depends on the group in question. Some quartets and choruses are more or less active year round, although this is more difficult to achieve in a quartet, where substitutes for vacationing members are seldom available.

9 Quoted in Shapiro and Hentoff, *Hear Me Talkin' to Ya*, 405.

Bibliography

Abbott, Lynn. '"Play That Barber Shop Chord": A Case for the African-American Origin of Barbershop Harmony.' *American Music* 10 (1992): 289–325.

Baker, Ella. '"Please Stop This Trend."' *The Harmonizer* 49 (July/August 1989): 28.

Becker, Howard S. *Art Worlds.* Berkeley: University of California Press, 1982.

Bishop, Jeff, and Paul Hoggett. *Organizing around Enthusiasms: Mutual Aid in Leisure.* London: Comedia Publishing Group, 1986.

Brandt, Max H. 'The Respectable Art of Woodshedding in World Music.' In *Barbershopping: Musical and Social Harmony,* edited by Max Kaplan, 33–54. Cranbury, N.J.: Associated University Presses, 1993.

Buchanan, T. 'Commitment and Leisure Behavior.' *Leisure Sciences* 7 (1985): 401–20.

Buerkle, Jack V., and Danny Barker. *Bourbon Street Black: The New Orleans Black Jazzman.* New York: Oxford University Press, 1973.

Collier, James L., and J. Bradford Robinson. 'Jazz.' In *The New Grove Dictionary of American Music.* Vol. 2, edited by H. Wiley Hitchcock and Stanley Sadie, 535–62. New York: Macmillan, 1986.

Csikszentmihalyi, Mihalyi. *Beyond Boredom and Anxiety: The Experience of Play in Work and Games.* San Francisco: Jossey-Bass, 1975.

Dawney, Michael. 'Tonsorial Musicians.' *Musical Opinion* 110 (1987): 208–9.

Dieringer Research Associates. 'A Report on Telephone Interviews with New Members of the Society for the Preservation and Encouragement of Barber Shop Quartet Singing in America.' Milwaukee, Wis., 1993.

– 'A Report on Telephone Interviews with the General Population Regarding Awareness of and Interest in The Society for the Preservation and Encouragement of Barber Shop Quartet Singing in America.' Milwaukee, Wis., 1993.

– 'Society for the Preservation and Encouragement of Barber Shop Quartet Singing in America, Inc., Chapter Study.' Vol. 1. Milwaukee, Wis., 1994.

Dumazedier, Joffre. 'Leisure and Postindustrial Societies.' In *Technology, Human*

Values, and Leisure, edited by Max Kaplan and Philip Bosserman. Nashville, Tenn.: Abington, 1971.

Fischer, Lucy. R., and Katherine B. Schaffer. *Older Volunteers: A Guide to Research and Practice.* Newbury Park, Calif.: Sage, 1993.

Foster, Dutton. 'Let's End "Put-Down" of Women in Our Performances.' *The Harmonizer* 49 (July/August 1989): 31.

Gates, J. Terry. 'A Historical Comparison of Public Singing by American Men and Women.' *Journal of Research in Music Education* 37 (1989): 32–46.

– 'Barbershoppers and Music Educators: Elitist/Populist Dualisms and the American Music Preservation Problem.' In *Barbershopping: Musical and Social Harmony*, edited by Max Kaplan, 95-107. Cranbury, N.J.: Associated University Presses, 1993.

Glaser, Barney L., and Anselm L. Strauss. *The Discovery of Grounded Theory.* Chicago: Aldine, 1967.

Glyptis, Sue. 'Lifestyles and Leisure Patterns – Methodological Approaches.' In *Life Styles: Theories, Concepts, Methods, and Results of Life Style Research in International Perspective.* Vol. 1, edited by Blanka Filipcova, Sue Glyptis, and Walter Tokarski, 37–67. Prague, Czechoslovakia: Academy of Sciences, 1989.

– *Leisure and Unemployment.* Milton Keynes, Eng.: Open University Press, 1989.

Goffman, Erving. *Stigma: Notes on the Management of Spoiled Identity.* Englewood Cliffs, N.J.: Prentice-Hall, 1963.

Hall, Richard H. 'Theoretical Trends in the Sociology of Occupations.' *The Sociological Quarterly* 24 (1983): 5–23.

Harmony, Inc. 'Harmony from Our Hearts: Harmony, Inc. 1959–1984.' N.p.: Harmony, Inc., 1985.

Hatton, Ken. 'A Little More Tonal Color, Please.' *The Harmonizer* 54 (September/October, 1994): 36.

Hicks, Val. 'Barbershop Quartet Singing.' In *The New Grove Dictionary of American Music.* Vol. 1, edited by H. Wiley Hitchcock and Stanley Sadie, 147. New York: Macmillan, 1986.

– ed. *Heritage of Harmony.* Kenosha, Wis.: SPEBSQSA, 1988.

Homans, George C. *Social Behavior: Its Elementary Forms.* Rev. ed. New York: Harcourt Brace Jovanovich, 1974.

Kaplan, Max. *Leisure: Theory and Policy.* New York: Wiley, 1975.

– 'SPEBSQSA's Future: Tradition and Innovation.' In *Barbershopping: Social and Musical Harmony*, edited by Max Kaplan, 126-44. Cranbury, N.J.: Associated University Presses, 1993.

– ed. *Barbershopping: Musical and Social Harmony.* Cranbury, N.J.: Associated University Presses, 1993.

Kelly, John R. 'Sociological Perspectives and Leisure Research.' *Current Sociology* 22 (1974): 127–58.
– *Leisure Identities and Interactions.* Boston: George Allen & Unwin, 1983.
Klegon, Douglas. 'The Sociology of Professions: An Emerging Perspective.' *Sociology of Work and Occupations* 5 (1978): 259–83.
Lewis, George H. 'The Sociology of Popular Culture.' *Current Sociology* 26/3 (1978): 1–160.
Lyman, Stanford M., and Marvin B. Scott. *A Sociology of the Absurd.* 2d ed. Dix Hills, N.J.: General Hall, 1989.
Machlis, Joseph. *The Enjoyment of Music.* 5th ed. New York: W.W. Norton, 1984.
Martin, Deac. 'The Evolution of Barbershop Harmony.' *1965 Music Journal Annual* (1965): 40–1, 106.
– *Book of Musical Americana.* Englewood Cliffs, N.J.: Prentice-Hall, 1970.
Neulinger, John. *To Leisure: An Introduction.* Boston: Allyn and Bacon, 1981.
Olmsted, A.D. 'Hobbies and Serious Leisure.' *World Leisure and Recreation* 35 (Spring, 1993): 27–32.
Parsons, Sandra. *30 Years of Harmony: Sweet Adelines, Inc., 1947–1977.* Tulsa, Okla.: Sweet Adelines, Inc., 1978.
Pavalko, Ronald M. *Sociology of Occupations and Professions.* 2d ed. Itasca, Ill.: F.E. Peacock, 1988.
The Pitch Pipe 42 (January, 1990): 16.
– 46 (January, 1994): inside front cover.
Podilchak, Walter. 'Distinctions of Fun, Enjoyment, and Leisure.' *Leisure Studies* 10 (1991): 133–48.
Randel, Don M. *The New Harvard Dictionary of Music.* Cambridge, Mass.: Belknap Press of Harvard University Press, 1986.
Ritzer, George, and David Walczak. *Working: Conflict and Change.* 3d ed. Englewood Cliffs, N.J.: Prentice-Hall, 1986.
Rosenthal, S.F. 'Marginal or Mainstream: Two Studies of Contemporary Chiropractic.' *Sociological Focus* 14 (1981): 271–85.
Select Committee on the Status and Future of the Society. 'A Strategic Plan for the Barbershop Harmony Society.' Kenosha, Wis.: SPEBSQSA, 1988.
Shamir, Boas. 'Commitment and Leisure.' *Sociological Perspectives* 31 (1988): 238–58.
Shapiro, Nat, and Nat Hentoff. *Hear Me Talkin' to Ya.* New York: Reinhart, 1955.
Snyder, Dean. 'Historical Notes.' *The Harmonizer* 40 (March/April, 1980): 20.
– 'Historical Notes.' *The Harmonizer* 42 (May/June, 1982): 14.
– 'From the Inside – A Descriptive View of SPEBSQSA.' In *Barbershopping: Musical*

and Social Harmony, edited by Max Kaplan, 13-32. Cranbury, N.J.: Associated University Presses, 1993.

Sobel, Michael E. *Lifestyle and Social Structure: Concepts, Definitions, Analyses.* New York: Academic Press, 1981.

Souchon, Edmond, and Al Rose. *New Orleans Jazz: A Family Album.* Rev. ed. Baton Rouge, La: Louisiana State University Press, 1978.

SPEBSQSA. 'Barbershop Arranging Manual.' Kenosha, Wis., 1980.

– 'The President.' Kenosha, Wis., 1989.

Sparkes, Wilbur, and David Wright. 'Barbershop Harmony: Where and How Did It All Begin?' *The Harmonizer* (parts 1 and 2) 49 (May/June, July/August, 1989): 18/14.

Stebbins, Robert A. 'A Theory of the Jazz Community.' *The Sociological Quarterly* 9 (1968): 318–31.

– 'Career: The Subjective Approach.' *The Sociological Quarterly* 11 (1970): 32–49.

– 'Music among Friends: The Social Networks of Amateur Classical Musicians.' *International Review of Sociology* (Series II) 12 (1976): 52–73.

– 'Classical Music Amateurs: A Definitional Study.' *Humboldt Journal of Social Relations* 5 (1978): 78–103.

– 'Creating High Culture: The American Amateur Classical Musician.' *Journal of American Culture* 1 (1978): 616–31.

– *Amateurs: On the Margin between Work and Leisure.* Beverly Hills, Calif.: Sage, 1979.

– 'Toward a Social Psychology of Stage Fright.' In *Sport in the Sociocultural Process*, edited by Marie Hart and Susan Birrell, 156–63. Dubuque, Iowa: W.C. Brown, 1981.

– 'Serious Leisure: A Conceptual Statement.' *Pacific Sociological Review* 25 (1982): 251–72.

– 'Amateur and Professional Astronomers: A Study of Their Interrelationships.' *Urban Life* 10 (1982): 433–54.

– *The Laugh-Makers: Stand-Up Comedy as Art, Business, and Life-Style.* Montreal and Kingston: McGill-Queen's University Press, 1990.

– *Amateurs, Professionals, and Serious Leisure.* Montreal and Kingston: McGill-Queen's University Press, 1992.

– 'Costs and Rewards in Barbershop Singing.' *Leisure Studies* 11 (1992): 123–33.

– *Career, Culture, and Social Psychology in a Variety Art: The Magician.* Malabar, Florida: Krieger, 1993.

– 'The Liberal Arts Hobbies: A Neglected Subtype of Serious Leisure.' *Loisir et Société/Society and Leisure* 17 (1994): 173–86.

– 'Lifestyle as a Generic Concept in Ethnographic Research.' Paper presented at the Qualitative Research Conference, University of Waterloo, Waterloo, Ontario, May, 1994.

– *The Connoisseur's New Orleans.* Calgary, Alta.: University of Calgary Press, 1995.
– *Tolerable Differences: Living with Deviance.* Toronto: McGraw-Hill Ryerson, 1996.
Strauss, Anselm L. *Qualitative Analysis for Social Scientists.* New York: Cambridge University Press, 1987.
Truzzi, Marcello. 'Toward A General Sociology of the Folk, Popular, and Elite Arts.' In *Research in Sociology of Knowledge, Sciences, and Art,* Vol. 1, edited by Robert A. Jones, 279–89. Greenwich, Conn.: JAI, 1978.
Unruh, David R. 'Characteristics and Types of Participation in Social Worlds.' *Symbolic Interactionism* 2 (1978): 115–30.
– 'The Nature of Social Worlds.' *Pacific Sociological Review* 23 (1980): 271–96.
Van Til, Jon. *Mapping the Third Sector: Voluntarism in a Changing Political Economy.* New York: The Foundation Center, 1988.
Veal, A.J. 'Leisure, Lifestyle and Status: A Pluralist Framework for Analysis.' *Leisure Studies* 8 (1989): 141–53.
– 'The Concept of Lifestyle: A Review.' *Leisure Studies* 12 (1993): 233–52.
Wardwell, Walter I. 'A Marginal Professional Role: The Chiropractor.' *Social Forces* 30 (1952): 339–48.
Zurcher, Louis A., Jr, R. George Kirkpatrick, Robert G. Cushing, and Charles K. Bowman. 'The Anti-Pornography Campaign: A Symbolic Crusade.' *Social Problems* 19 (1971): 217–38.

Index